HELPING
THE
HURTING
IN YOUR
CHURCH

HELPING
THE
HURTING
IN YOUR
CHURCH

DR. STEVEN L. DOWDLE

CREATION
HOUSE
A STRANG COMPANY

HELPING THE HURTING IN YOUR CHURCH by Dr. Steven L. Dowdle
Published by Creation House
A Strang Company
600 Rinehart Road
Lake Mary, Florida 32746
www.creationhouse.com

Cover design by Terry Clifton

Library of Congress Control Number: 2006939055
International Standard Book Number: 978-1-59979-163-0

First Edition

07 08 09 10 11 — 9 8 7 6 5 4 3 2 1
Printed in the United States of America

This book is dedicated to all the pastors and lay helpers who serve faithfully in providing "soul care" for those who are hurting in their congregations.

CONTENTS

ACKNOWLEDGMENTS

This project could not have been completed without the encouragement and support of the pastoral team of Casas. Senior Pastor Roger Barrier was eager to have our story, and the lessons learned over twenty-six years of ministry together, recorded for future generations of Casas pastors and for all pastors, young and old, in the ministry. Initially the story begins with him and his desire after three years in his first full-time pastorate, to help those who came to a small, but rapidly growing church, for help with their personal concerns. The helpers who followed included: pastors, counselors, lay helpers, elders, intercessors, and support staff who shaped the ministry with their contributions and spiritual gifts.

I owe a special thanks to the following who read and critiqued chapters: Rev. Maureen Brand, Rev. Bill Calkins, Dr. Randy Carlson, Dr. Jim Corcoran, Dr. Larry Hagberg, Anne Lewis, Pat Lutz, Rev. Tom Machamer, Karen Machamer, Dawn Martin, Richard Murphy, Nelda Nichols, Rev. Randy Reynolds, Rev. Gary Shrader, Rev. Jerry Wilkinson, and Rev. Evelyn Wright.

I am thankful to all who courageously shared their pain and suffering with us, and, in doing so, allowed us to learn of the power of the healing work of Jesus Christ and to witness the Holy Spirit at work among us.

FOREWORD

When I left the pastorate to teach at Talbot School of Theology, I went with the realization that there were people in the church who had problems that I didn't have answers for, and that really bothered me. I believed that Christ was the answer and His truth set people free, but I really didn't know how to minister that in a life-changing and liberating way. At the seminary, I offered a masters of theology elective on resolving personal and spiritual conflicts. In reality, I was searching for answers to people's problems, and God started to send hurting Christians to see me.

I believed then, and I do now, that our problems are physical, psychological, and spiritual, and I wanted an answer that was holistic and biblically balanced. I have since been on a journey of discovering the omnipresence of God and His desire to see captives set free and the brokenhearted healed and restored in Christ. At the time when I first sensed God's leading to go public with what I had learned, Casas Adobes Baptist Church in Tucson, Arizona asked me to do a conference at their church.

I discovered there a godly pastoral staff that was on the same journey I was. This wonderful core of believers is still together after more than twenty years of ministry. That is a powerful testimony of what pastoral relationships should be, as led by Senior Pastor Dr. Roger Barrier. What you are about to read is a valuable contribution to the ministry of pastoral care on the local church level. Steve Dowdle and his staff have long since moved away from secular psychology and discovered a biblical psychology that recognizes Jesus as the Wonderful Counselor and Great Physician. He presents a strategic model of caring for all the needs of a congregation that draws from many resources in the body of Christ. I am confident that you will be blessed as you read this timely book and seek to use this tool to help many in your church discover their identity and freedom in Christ through genuine repentance and faith in God.

—DR. NEIL T. ANDERSON, PRESIDENT
DISCIPLESHIP COUNSELING MINISTRIES

INTRODUCTION

Thirty-five pastors from our Tucson Barnabas Group sat in rapt attention as Dr. Steve Dowdle detailed the four types of people that pastors can't help. Before Steve's lecture, we all imagined that we could help everybody! Now, we knew we were wrong…and why.

Recognition lights were almost visible over each head as Steve detailed the four most common personality disorders that we were likely to encounter in our congregations. Not long into Steve's talk, I realized that I was connecting faces of some people I knew to the traits of the four groups he described. Listening to Steve, I understood why those people dominated 80 to 90 percent of my time—and why I never made successful headway with any of them.

I wish you could have been there with us that day. Not only did Steve outline these people who are difficult (if not impossible) to work with, he also told us why they were beyond pastoral help. We learned why these people drained us and so often hurt us, and the church, so badly. Fortunately, he did not leave us wondering what to do next. He gave careful guidelines on how to minimize their destructive influence while sharing the few things we could do to open an avenue of genuine help to them.

Steve and I have been friends and cohorts in the ministry at the same church for almost thirty years. I was a fortunate pastor because seldom did I have to go through difficult crises or people problems alone. Steve's counseling office was just around the corner!

One of our early church mottos was, "Helping hurting people." A ministry market always exists for a church that sets its heart on helping hurting people. The world is full of them, and over the years God has sent us an abundance of people needing our help.

During these years we have dealt with almost every problem a pastor might encounter: from benevolence to demonic bondage; from sexual abuse to abandonment; from mood disorders to murders; from sickness to suicide; from adultery to incest; from divorce to imprisonment; from tax evasion to bankruptcy. There might be things we have not faced, but I can't think of any!

Steve has carefully directed the contents of this book to pastors of all ages and circumstances who welcome help in dealing with the difficult issues that people bring into the pastor's office—often unannounced and uncalled for! Young pastors in small churches who are doing everything alone, snowed under by requests from people, and sometimes without help will find special encouragement in these pages, along with insight and relevant tools for helping hurting people.

My prayer is that the Lord will anoint this collection of Steve's consolidated wisdom and experience to be a blessing both to the pastoral ministry in the kingdom and to the many people who are struggling every day to make life work—and as best I can see, that includes all of us. Amen.

—ROGER BARRIER, SENIOR PASTOR
CASAS ADOBES BAPTIST CHURCH

CHAPTER 1

PASTORAL CARE IN HISTORICAL PERSPECTIVE

I was just sitting down to supper when the phone rang. The call was from Roger Barrier, senior pastor at Casas Adobes Baptist Church, asking me to accompany him to the hospital. He had just received a panicked call from the grandfather of a sixteen-month-old baby girl. Through his tears, the man told Roger that his granddaughter had just been rushed to the emergency room due to a drowning accident and was not expected to live.

When we arrived at the ER, we were told that the baby had indeed died. The hospital staff directed us to the distraught father, who was sitting on the curb outside of the ER, his face buried in his hands. As pastors, we were faced with the awesome responsibility and strategic opportunity of bringing comfort to this hurting man. As we shared this tragic and horrifying moment with the grieving family, we linked their suffering with the reality of the compassion Jesus Christ had for them. And in so doing, we were also linked to a long heritage of pastors meeting the needs of wounded sheep within the body of Christ.

Pastors have been ministering to hurting people under their care throughout Christian history. As we consider the role of the pastor as a caregiver in its twenty-first-century context, an understanding of the history of pastoral care will put the church's response to the needs of its people in previous centuries into perspective. The biblical record, as well as a study of church history, reveals that the human condition has not changed over time.

People continue to need comfort in times of grief, guidance in times of confusion, direction in times of wandering, healing in times of suffering, reconciliation in times of conflict, and admonishment in times of disobedience. Pastoral care, or soul care, has been and continues to be one of the primary functions of the pastor. It links the pastor of today with the pastor of yesterday. Pastoral care has a rich history developed by our pastoral forebears and practiced from the first century onward with a desire to bring the comfort of Jesus to hurting and suffering people.

In AD 590, Gregory, a Benedictine monk, wrote his seminal treatise, *Pastoral Care.* This book became the primary resource for defining what effective soul care might entail for the parish priest or pastor. For one thousand years of church history, it set the standard for the vocabulary, methods, and goals, and established the norm for caring for hurting people. Gregory was very explicit in how a pastor was to handle individual cases. He was thorough as he gave his direction, which distinguished between men and women; the young and the old; the poor and the rich; the slothful and the hasty; the meek and the choleric; the humble and the haughty; the kindly and the envious. He identified thirty-seven categories of people classifications and gave specific counsel on how to admonish each of them.[1]

He also wrote about the demands of the role of the pastor and the requirements of the office. He addressed the importance of the inner and outer life of the pastor being consistently holy and pure before the Lord. He urged pastors to be aware of their own weaknesses and to humbly deal with them in prayer and personal discipline. This book was esteemed for centuries by bishops and priests. In AD 796, Eanbald, the Archbishop of York, was advised by a colleague: "Wherever you go, let the pastoral book of St. Gregory be your companion. Read and re-read it often, that in it you may learn to know yourself and your work, that you may have before your eyes how you ought to live and teach. The book is a mirror of the life of a bishop and medicine for all the wounds inflicted by the Devil's deception."[2] At one point in history it was customary to give a copy of this book to all new bishops at their consecration, and they were admonished in the ceremony "to observe this Rule in their life, their teaching and their Pastoral decisions."[3]

Throughout church history, leaders have addressed the pastoral responsibility of caring for the needs of their people. Clement, for example, wrote and probably preached a sermon to the second century church at Corinth known as "The Second Epistle of Clement." His major purpose was to encourage local pastors to assist troubled people by urging and admonishing them to deal with their issues with "great purity of life" in light of the impending end of the world.[4]

Cyprian wrote to the people of Thibaris in about AD 250 on how to face and deal with martyrdom. John Chrysostom gave classic counsel to a young widow on how to deal with grief.[5] The puritan scholar, pastor, and writer Richard Baxter (1615–1691) wrote his famous *A Christian Directory* in 1665, which he described as a "sum of practical theology."[6] In Part II of this monumental work, he deals with marriage, parenting, family worship, personal devotions, and many other subjects relevant to the application of Christian values and biblical teaching to daily life.

J. I. Packer, who wrote an introduction for the 1996 reprint of Baxter's book, states: "modern readers will be fascinated to see how in this book things that are culturally quaint and idiosyncratic blend with what is spiritually profound and wise." He goes on to describe Baxter's work as, "the fullest, most thorough, most profound treatment of Christian spirituality and standards that has ever been attempted by an English-speaking evangelical author."[7] Baxter's work illustrates from a seventeenth-century perspective an effort to establish a norm for pastors to follow in terms of helping people to understand how they are to relate to God and to each other. He established the foundation upon which our pastoral emphasis on marriage and family life rests.

Baxter framed for us the view that God made us to fulfill the two great commandments: to love Him and to love our neighbors as we love ourselves; and further that loving others must begin in the home. Baxter taught that he who fails to love his spouse and children as himself remains a hypocrite and a failed disciple regardless of how much he works in the church. We can identify many of the values that govern our counsel as the same ones Baxter taught in the seventeenth century. The contributions of these men are unequaled and certainly foundational in establishing the way we care for our people.

In their book *Pastoral Care in Historical Perspective*, Clebsh and Jaekle help us to see pastoral care from a macro viewpoint. They identified four pastoral functions that have been distinct and consistently operative in church life for centuries. These four functions of pastoral care—the care of souls—are:

- *Healing*—the restoration of a person to a condition of wholeness with the assumption that this restoration also achieves a new level of spiritual insight and welfare.

- *Sustaining*—the helping of a hurting person to endure and transcend a circumstance in which restoration to his former condition or recuperation from his malady is either impossible or so remote as to seem improbable. The sustaining function normally employs the means of compassionate commiseration—it attempts to achieve spiritual growth through endurance of unwanted, harmful, or dangerous experiences. Perhaps the most common form of sustaining is found in the pastoral ministry to bereaved persons.

- *Guiding*—the assisting of perplexed persons to make confident choices between alternative courses of thought and action when such choices are viewed as affecting the present and future state of the soul.

- *Reconciling*—the seeking to reestablish broken relationships between men and between man and God. Reconciliation employs two emphatic modes of operation, which we call forgiveness and discipline. Classically, Christian pastoral care has employed the mode of forgiveness in the sacramental acts of confession and absolution, both of which aim at amendment of life and the restoration of right relations with God and with neighbor. Discipline,

> on the other hand, serves as a mode of reconciliation
> by placing alienated persons into situations in which
> good relationships might be reestablished.[8]

Clebsh and Jaekle described these four functions in detail and how they have been applied at different times throughout church history. Healing, for example, has been administered through the use of prayer, oil, herbs, medicines, relics, shrines, exorcism, and vows. Sustaining has used prayer, holy objects, and regulations and has led to numerous writings on how to deal with the sufferings of life and death. Guiding has employed the written advice of experts as well as counseling techniques. Reconciling also used sacramental means and ritual, including confession, repentance, and working through forgiveness of others. The authors point out that while pastors performed all four functions in every period of Christian history, "each specific period reveals one or another function, or mode of performing that function, to have been practiced so pervasively or with such fascination that an era may be characterized by it."[9] They describe eight epochs in the history of Christian pastoring and identify which function was dominant in each. A brief description of each of these epochs is provided to enhance our macro view of the scope of pastoral care over the centuries.

> ▸ Primitive Christianity—The first era of pastoral care
> lasted until about AD 180 and was characterized by
> an emphasis on sustaining souls as the world moved
> swiftly toward what they perceived as its end.

> ▸ Under Oppression—In the era of persecution from
> about AD 180–306, the function of reconciling

troubled people to God and to the church became more important than the function of sustaining. During these decades, pastors labored hard to codify major sins and describe their appropriate penalties.

▶ Christian Culture—This period was characterized by guiding people to behave in accord with the norms of the newly-established Christian culture. This period began when Christianity became a legal religion under Constantine and continued through the Byzantine period.

▶ Dark Ages—In the West, the church's encounter with the Teutonic peoples of northern Europe quickly polarized soul care around inductive guidance.

▶ Medieval Christendom—This period brought about a codification of pastoral care around a well-defined sacramental system designed to heal all of the maladies that beset any segment of common life.

▶ Renewal and Reform—The rise of individualism in the Renaissance and Reformation periods thrust reconciling into a prominence unknown before or since that era.

▶ Enlightenment—In the Enlightenment, Christian pastoring sharply focused on sustaining souls as they passed through the treacheries and pitfalls of a threatening, wicked world.

▶ Post-Christendom Era—The emphasis of the late nineteenth and twentieth centuries tends toward guidance that "endures values and norms from personal convictions and value systems." This era has witnessed the rise of nonpastoral professions capable of healing, sustaining, guiding, and reconciling troubled individuals.[10]

Clebsh and Jaekle pointed out that in the modern era, pastoral care has been moved into a junior partner role to other, nonministerial helping professions. But it is this author's opinion and observation that "soul care" has moved up in stature among the helping professions since Clebsh and Jaekle wrote their book in 1975 and revised it in 1983. Presently, I believe we are seeing movement to defining our identity in pastoral care as distinct and separate, yet aligned with psychology, psychiatry, counseling, and social work for the benefit of hurting people. A prime example of this rise in stature is the emergence of the American Association of Christian Counselors (AACC). The focus of this professional organization on training, education, spiritual development, and the integration of prayer therapy and counseling marks a return of the church, albeit in the context of psychological professionalism, to its historical roots of caring for hurting people both spiritually and emotionally.

The Christian Association for Psychological Studies has, since the mid-1950s, guided the integration of faith and practice for thousands of Christian mental health workers who were trained professionally in secular programs. It is these Christian mental health workers who have been the prime movers in bringing about the reuniting of the church and its historic role as people helpers with the nonpastoral professions and their passion for helping people toward health.

It is within this historical context that this book on pastoral care is written. The experiences of our church staff in developing our strategy for caring for people are remarkably similar to those of pastors who ministered centuries ago. We are driven by the same concern and compassion as those who came before us to see the ministry of Jesus bring healing and restoration to the human condition.

CHAPTER 2

A CONTEMPORARY PERSPECTIVE: THE CASAS STORY

The Casas story is unique in many respects. It is a departure from the norm for our denomination, and, indeed, a departure from the norm for most evangelical churches. It is the story of a spiritual pilgrimage for our staff and lay leaders that resulted in the stretching of our preconceptions and the molding of a biblical worldview. When the church hired this author as its first staff counselor, none of us knew the direction the counseling ministry would take. What we discovered was that hurting people brought their issues, concerns, and pain to us with the expectation that we would have answers to their spiritual questions, as well as with the understanding that we would be able to help them with their emotional and relational pain.

These people brought a spiritual hunger to the counseling sessions that I, as a secularly-trained counselor, was challenged to respond to in a way that addressed that spiritual dimension, as well as the relational and emotional dimension of the situation. It was (and still is) the expectation of those who bring their hurts to the church that the church would be able to connect them with God in the midst of their suffering. It is the expectation of the hurting that the church and the counseling pastor will have answers and a sense of direction to guide them through their suffering.

These are some of the difficult questions posed to me in the early years of establishing a spiritually viable counseling ministry in the church:

- If God really loves me, why did my healthy four-year-old suddenly die of a brain aneurysm?

- Where was Jesus when I was being raped?

- Why did God allow my husband to succumb to an affair and lose his pastorate?

- Could my problem with depression be caused by demonic oppression?

- Would you pray for my physical healing?

- I was ritually abused as a child. Can you help me?

- I do not trust God or any man! Can you help me build trust?

- Is there any hope that I will ever be able to lead a normal Christian life?

▸ I can't sit in the worship service. It drives me crazy! I can't really understand what the pastor is talking about in his sermons, and I really can't see the words on the pages of the Bible when he reads Scripture. What do you think is going on?

What we discovered as we began our church counseling ministry was that as the "patients" came to the "emergency room" of the "spiritual hospital," they assumed we would have spiritually-sound, biblically-based answers and strategies to help them deal with their concerns. The challenge faced by our staff and others in the then-emerging field of Christian counseling in 1979, was to integrate our knowledge and training from secular academic programs with our biblical knowledge and understanding. Those of us "in the trenches" had to work hard to accelerate this learning process while at the same time dealing daily with the difficult issues and questions posed by those we were trying to help.

In our situation, this process was compounded by the persistent high demand for counseling in the setting of a rapidly growing church filled with new believers. The dual pressures exerted by this high demand and the incomplete integration of secular and spiritual counseling models forced us to move forward faster than was comfortable for any of us. It was, however, this pressure that forced us to grow, experiment, and learn through the application of new knowledge and experience. The difficult questions clients brought to the counseling sessions were great motivators to seek what God was asking us to learn to help them.

The needs of clients were also catalytic in the development of multiple ministries at Casas. The benevolence ministry was established to address the financial needs of our church people, as well as the needs of others in our community. Our annual benevolence offering is now the third largest designated item in our church budget, exceeded only by our building and missions funds. We will deal with this ministry in detail in chapter 10. The needs of single parents, revealed in the counseling process, helped to initiate specific ministries to them to address their financial and emotional needs. A single mom's car clinic was a big hit, as men volunteered their time on a Saturday morning to change oil and do minor car repairs. A special fund was set up to help with the financial needs of single mothers, and classes were offered to support them as they parented alone.

The need for a support structure that went beyond the counseling relationship became obvious as we worked with those struggling with various addictions. After using Christian 12 Step material for a number of years, we selected the Celebrate Recovery program, developed by Saddleback Community Church in Lake Forest, California. We are in our third year of offering this comprehensive approach to helping people overcome their unhealthy ways of coping with life. We will address this program in more detail in chapter 7.

A prayer ministry evolved out of our desire to respond to clients' needs for spiritual and emotional healing. We will discuss this ministry in our next chapter. These ministries provide a support network within the church that allows us to comprehensively and more effectively respond to the needs of our people. As a result of these ministries, Casas is recognized in the community as a church that helps hurting people. In our counseling ministry alone, we have ministered to more than sixteen thousand individuals in the past twenty-six years.

The field of Christian counseling emerged in its infancy at the same time we were developing our approach to helping hurting people. We were able to benefit from the contributions of authors like James Dobson, Norm Wright, David Seamons, Clyde Narramore, and William Backus. The Christian Association for Psychological Studies provided an opportunity for dialogue and learning in these early years of our ministry. This first period in our counseling ministry, from 1979–1989, was marked by an effort to assimilate, integrate, refine, purge, and build our worldview. As the ministry progressed, our goal was always that it be in its essence a biblical ministry.

We faced another challenge in addition to our attempts to integrate secular training with a spiritual model of counseling. In keeping with our tradition as Baptists, the role of the Holy Spirit and the supernatural intervention of God in people's lives had not been a major emphasis. Most traditional Baptists had been influenced by the cessationism of John Calvin, "who did not believe in a healing ministry or deliverance."[1] Another influence was the writings of William Barclay, who, in his commentary on Matthew 8:28–34, implied that the demon-possessed men only *believed* they were under the influence of demonic forces and therefore acted accordingly.[2] He described Jesus as restoring their sanity rather than delivering them from demonic bondage.

John Darby, who developed the doctrine of dispensationalism in the mid-1800s, influenced the thinking and belief of generations of pastors and teachers. He proposed that the supernatural gifts of the spirit "were intended for the special dispensation of apostolic times."[3] Darby influenced D. L. Moody and C. I. Scofield to his way of interpreting Scripture when it came to the supernatural work of the Holy Spirit.[4] These two men, through the Moody Bible Institute and the Scofield Reference Bible respectively, influenced thousands of pastors and teachers in the conservative-evangelical tradition to regard healing with suspicion, if not outright hostility.

Like most evangelicals, we had to struggle with balancing what we had been taught in light of what we were experiencing. As we counseled and prayed with hurting people, we clearly saw that God was working in their lives in ways that could only be explained by His power. It was therefore incumbent upon us to learn as much as we could about what the Bible actually said (as opposed to the teachings of tradition) about how the Holy Spirit worked and wanted to express Himself in the context of helping people deal with their suffering. We faced difficult questions like those listed earlier in this chapter with a sense of inadequacy. This was based on the shortcomings of our secular education and the deficits in our biblical understanding and experience with the supernatural work of the Lord Jesus through the Holy Spirit.

What we discovered was that the Holy Spirit had not ceased His ministry of healing and deliverance at the end of the apostolic age, but that throughout church history He had been doing the work of Jesus Christ to heal and deliver.[5] Fortunately, others were dealing with the same process and were writing and teaching on the ministry of the Holy Spirit. John Wimber, Peter Wagner, Derek Prince, Frances McNutt, Jack Deere, John White, Mark Bubeck, Dennis and Matthew Linn, Neil Anderson, and Charles Kraft offered guidance and teaching. Their work was a godsend for those of us in ministry to the hurting. We were also blessed to work in a spiritually and intellectually free environment in which a process of investigation, questioning, and experimentation with our emerging new biblical worldview could take place.

It is important to note that this process was shared by the professional counselors, pastoral staff, and lay leadership of the church. While the thrust of the process emanated from the counseling ministry and its desire to be spiritually powerful as well as professionally effective, the process of changing our worldview was an inclusive one. Both the lay and pastoral leadership worked together and in concert with the counselors to ensure a solid foundation for our ministry. Without this synergy of effort and desire to follow God's leading, we would have been unable to achieve the level of effectiveness we are now experiencing.

It must also be acknowledged that it was often the penetrating and frequently pain-filled questions brought to us by hurting people that provided the catalyst for this pilgrimage of faith and service. As leaders of Casas, we wanted to be facilitators of bringing the authority of Jesus Christ to bear on the sufferings of His people and to rejoice together in the victories won by His power. It is this legacy that we want to leave for future generations of pastoral and lay leaders at Casas, and to share with the church at large. Our pilgrimage has defined who we are and revealed who God wanted us to be. It shaped our "spiritual DNA" and clearly focused our identity within our doctrinal tradition.[6] We have experienced and believe the following:

▸ The authority of Jesus Christ over the destructive work of the enemy in the lives of God's people. We accept as reality that the enemy has established footholds in the lives of God's people and that Jesus came to set the captives free. (See Ephesians 4:26–27.)

▸ The relevant urgency for the use of spiritual gifts, as they are given for the edification of the body of Christ and most notably the gifts of discernment, knowledge, wisdom, healing, encouragement, mercy, and prophecy in our healing and counseling ministries. (See 1 Corinthians 12; Ephesians 4; and Romans 12.)

▸ The supernatural work of the Holy Spirit in healing the body and soul. We bear witness to the presence of the Holy Spirit in the continuing work of Jesus in healing and deliverance. We acknowledge our dependence on the Holy Spirit to do His work through us, and place our faith in Him and not in our own limited knowledge and experience. We rely on His direct intervention and participation in each counseling and prayer session.

▸ The value in recognizing that neuroscience and psychology have much to offer us in our understanding of how to help people, and that it is possible to integrate that knowledge with the spiritual process of healing and restoration. We acknowledge that God's truth should not be divided and labeled as secular or sacred, for He is the Creator of the universe and all that is in it.

▸ The continuing work of Jesus Christ through the Holy Spirit to empower, admonish, heal, deliver, convict, lead, and teach; and our responsibility as a church to actively participate in this ongoing ministry of Jesus Christ. It is important for us to acknowledge in our teaching and our praying that everything we do is done under the authority and direction of the Holy Spirit, and that we are servants in submission to Him as He accomplishes His ministry through us.

It has been important to us to maintain balance in our approach to helping hurting people. As a church, we learned early in our journey to be willing to learn from others, to do our research, and to adapt our methodologies to fit our biblical position, our doctrinal comfort zone, and our church culture. We have found that working together on teams allowed us to capture the synergy of spiritual giftings, spiritual maturity, and personal experience necessary to maintain balance of perspective and practice. We found that working in teams that included people with spiritual gifts that would complement one another was effective in maintaining balance and focus. For example, forming teams with members who had the gifts of discernment, wisdom, and knowledge proved profitable in the difficult process of accurately diagnosing the causes of a person's suffering.

We learned to be very cautious about pronouncing a healing or revelation as being from God until it could be verified and confirmed by others. In the case of physical healing, it is important to have medical verification in order to preserve the integrity and credibility of the healing ministry. We have learned that the development of spiritual gifts seems to prosper in the confidential, trusting environment of a small prayer group. It is in this setting that we found that spiritual gifts, like physical muscles, can be exercised and strengthened through practice and repetition. (See Hebrews 5:14.) A natural check and balance evolves as individuals prayerfully experiment with what they believe God is showing them, and receive confirmation and encouragement of their brothers and sisters.

It is vitally important to establish a climate of humility among those with gifts like discernment and knowledge. We recognized that when gifted people act independently of supervision and accountability, they were often easily deceived and subject to prideful actions. Praying and ministering together consistently over time is effective in protecting those called to counseling ministry. A confidence and maturity in the exercise of one's gifts can be achieved in this kind of "safe" environment that is unlikely to occur in a more independent setting.

Prayer groups were organized, as those called to counseling ministry were identified, screened, and placed in a group by the supervising pastor. In our case, there have been as many as sixteen such groups, with six to ten intercessors in each. It is from these prayer groups that we have drawn people to form teams to pray with specific individuals or to pray over physical locations like homes, businesses, and our church property.

The prayer model we use has undergone many changes over the years. We evolved from the traditional Wednesday night prayer service to a multifaceted prayer ministry. We have called corporate prayer meetings for special situations, established a prayer room with a book of requests, called for *40 Days of Prayer* for the church at large, and developed a twenty-four-hour prayer hotline manned by 336 volunteers. Yet with all of these prayer programs, the small prayer group remains the cornerstone of our church prayer life and ministry. These small groups provide both the prayer cover we need as a church and the manpower to meet individual and corporate requests for prayer.

We have also discovered over the years that it is vital to maintain good communication between the prayer groups and the pastoral leadership. Our church organization structure provides for an associate pastor to oversee the pastoral care department, which includes the counseling, prayer, healing, and spiritual warfare ministries. This administrative oversight and connection to the chief operational body of the church allows for a two-way flow of communication. It is understood that when prayer groups believe they have spiritual insights that may be helpful for the pastoral leadership, they communicate them through the associate pastor, who in turn relays the messages to the pastoral leadership in the meetings he attends.

The roles of the prayer groups and the leadership are clearly defined. It is the duty of those praying (the "pray-ers") to listen, pray, and share when they are led to do so. It is the duty of those in pastoral leadership to confirm the content of the message and to make the decisions that may be necessary as a result of the information.

Often a prayer concern from a small group serves as a warning sign for the pastoral leadership. Many times they have joined a prayer group in praying about the issue or concern and significant operational decisions have been made as a result. Because we have a staff-led leadership style in our church, this interface between lay prayer groups and the pastoral leadership provides an important link both spiritually and operationally in bringing a degree of accountability and balance to the leadership and management process.

The Casas experience has also been one of learning from our mistakes and our lack of knowledge. Early in our ministry to those in spiritual bondage, we (both staff and lay leadership) were focused intently on our desire to help the oppressed. As a result, we neglected to lay a foundation by teaching on spiritual warfare to prepare the church for a ministry to the oppressed. We also failed to organize prayer support for those involved in the ministry. To compound the problem, we moved too fast, assuming everyone would see the need in the same way we saw it. As a result, opposition was organized against the ministry within the church body. Those who opposed praying for the deliverance of people who were oppressed by the enemy did so because of their belief that Christians cannot be "possessed" by demonic forces.

To them, praying for people who are professing Christians and yet claim to have demonic problems was nothing short of heresy. The term *possessed* is certainly problematic for many evangelicals. After careful study, it is our understanding that the Greek word commonly translated "possessed" in Matthew 8:16, 9:32, and Mark 1:32 and other passages is not well expressed by that rendering. A more accurate representation of what the writers intended would be better expressed by the word *demonized*, carrying the meaning of "to have a demon." The English word *possessed* implies ownership, a concept foreign to the New Testament discussion of demonic activity, and a concept that has no support in the Greek text.

The use of the word *possessed* greatly overstates the influence and power of the demonic. Satan and his demons own absolutely nothing. They are squatters—intruders subject to eviction at any time by the rightful Owner of everything. (See Psalm 24:1.) It is our position that a Christian cannot be possessed (owned) by a demon. A Christian can, however, be demonized—that is to be attacked, harassed, oppressed by (a) demon(s). Fuller Seminary professor Dr. Charles Kraft presents a thorough defense of deliverance ministries and this position on demonic power in his book, *Confronting Powerless Christianity*.[7]

Those who organized the opposition within the church to the healing and deliverance ministry wanted the leadership held accountable for leading the church in this direction and threatened the senior pastor and the associate pastor for pastoral care with the loss of their jobs. This crisis was used by God to show us the importance of preparing our people for ministries that move them out of their church tradition and doctrinal comfort zones. In response to this crisis, we formed a study committee composed of elders, staff, and lay leaders and took a year to carefully research the subject of spiritual warfare. At the conclusion of that study, this group brought to the church a recommendation on how we felt led to respond to the need for healing and deliverance ministries in our church. We included in our study writers on both sides of the issue of the relevance and propriety of ministry to the spiritually oppressed.

Our study led us to align with those who believe in the ongoing work of Jesus to heal and deliver the oppressed through the active work of the Holy Spirit. After studying various approaches to dealing with the demonic, we concluded that the power-encounter model of confronting the demonic—which we had previously used—was not the best approach for us. Instead, we selected the truth-encounter model that was being used by Talbot Seminary professor, Dr. Neil Anderson. We adopted this approach in dealing with demonic attacks in the lives of Christians because it places the responsibility for evicting the influence of the enemy on the individual, rather than on those leading the prayer session. It was also consistent with our understanding of Christian discipleship as requiring confession of sin and renunciation of the devil as a part of the maturation process. Dr. Anderson's seven steps to freedom provides the structure for the individual prayer sessions at the heart of this process.[8] They will be discussed in more detail in chapter 4.

As a result of this careful, balanced, and much slower approach, we were convinced of God's leadership to maintain a healing and deliverance ministry. The leadership asked the church to vote on whether they also discerned the same leadership by the Holy Spirit in this matter. A vote was taken during our Sunday morning services in 1989, and 96 percent of the congregation approved the proposal to move forward with a ministry to those under spiritual attack and in need of healing prayer. This gave us the unity we needed to effectively minister and experience the flow of the Holy Spirit. Our experience taught us that disunity and conflict block the Holy Spirit's ability to work freely in a congregation and provide the enemy with fertile ground in which to do his destructive work. Those who opposed the ministry left our church to go elsewhere. The staff remained intact and unified.

We learned a valuable lesson about the importance of spiritual unity within the body of Christ, especially as it relates to a frontline spiritual warfare ministry. We also learned the importance of doing our "homework" and being prepared to give a studied answer to those who have questions. We now offer what we call "core classes"—Principles of Spiritual Growth, Spiritual Warfare, Spiritual Gifts (SHAPE), Stewardship (Crown Ministries), and Evangelism—which are designed to teach our people what we believe as a church. This gives them an opportunity to participate in a classroom setting of healthy dialogue and discussion and provides them with the biblical and philosophical underpinnings for the ministries of the church. Sunday morning sermons have also been a vehicle through which the majority of the church membership have been taught and challenged to examine the theology foundational of our identity as a church.

We have identified three streams of theology which have helped shape Casas's unique call and identity, and upon which our teaching, ministry, and programs are grounded:

1. **A biblical theology of relationships** that views the Great Commandment (Mark 12:28–34) as the foundational imperative upon which all

doctrine and moral-ethical behavior depend. The hermeneutic associated with relational theology provides direction for a biblical interpretation that is essential to all preaching and teaching at Casas.

2. **A biblical theology of sanctification** that flows from the Keswick tradition. The primary tenets of this view of experiential sanctification include:

    A. Spiritual maturity moves us steadily toward an intimate relationship with God.
    B. The triune God is an active Participant in the process.
    C. The member must unconditionally surrender to the work of God in his life.
    D. The faith community plays a vital role in the individual's growth toward spiritual maturity.
    E. The result of the experiential sanctification is Christlikeness that is manifested in loving service to people and in the evangelizing of nonbelievers.

3. **A biblical theology of spiritual warfare** that recognizes the preeminent position of Jesus Christ as exalted by God to the highest place and given all power and authority over the work of the devil.

The Casas experience is one that is Spirit led, ongoing, and ever changing as we fine-tune our theological understanding and gain more experience in applying it to the needs of people. As you read about how we minister to the hurting and the oppressed in the chapters ahead, keep in mind that what is shared here is not meant to communicate that ours is the best or only approach. It is one church's experience, shared for the common good of the body of Christ. Every church must prayerfully consider what God is leading it to do. Casas is still a work in progress, and we continue to change and learn. We have not arrived at a point when we can say, "We are the experts—follow us!" We simply share what we have learned with the prayer that it will be an encouragement to you and your church to seek your own unique design, style, and focus under the leadership of the Holy Spirit. What a great privilege it is to be facilitators of the continuing work of Jesus Christ in preaching the good news of the gospel, setting the captives free, giving sight to the blind, releasing the oppressed, and victoriously proclaiming the year of God's favor in the lives of His people!

CHAPTER 3

AN INTEGRATIVE MODEL: HEALING PRAYER AND COUNSELING

A s Casas grew from a Sunday morning worship attendance of five hundred in 1979 to more than three thousand one hundred in 2005, we saw a large increase in the number of people seeking help from the counseling ministry. It became obvious to us that our knowledge and ability to address the woundedness of so many hurting people at the level necessary to see significant change in their lives was limited. We studied the ministry of Jesus, as recorded in the Gospels, read many books on healing and deliverance, and began to flesh out our approach to bring people to the Lord for healing. We viewed our role as being the stretcher bearers who carried the wounded to a place of healing.

We came to realize that without God's direct intervention into the lives of His people, there is little hope of permanent change at any level taking place. Our lack of experience and our ignorance of the role of the Holy Spirit in healing of body and soul, slowed our progress, but did not deter us from seeking a fuller understanding of His work. We were like beginner swimmers in the water, staying at the shallow (safe) end of the pool. Little by little we began to let go of the side of the pool as we gained the confidence and skill to move into deeper waters. We benefited from the contributions of many staff and lay leaders as this process took place.

We began to see healing from a more comprehensive and macro perspective, recognizing that wounded people need healing on multiple levels and at multiple points of woundedness within those levels. We reached the following conclusions as we "jumped into the deep end of the pool" and began to bring people to the Lord in prayer.

A significant number of Christians need emotional, spiritual, relational, and physical healing. The church in general, and pastors, counselors, and pray-ers specifically, are unaware of the extent of this need and therefore have no strategic approach to deal with it.

The evangelical church in general (and our church specifically) is weak in its theology of suffering and in the practical application of a theology of healing. The ministry of Jesus to heal and deliver His people continues today through the ministry of the Holy Spirit, and we want to be a part of what God desires to do in us and through us. The experiencing of God's love, mercy, and grace through healing—physically, emotionally, spiritually, and relationally—is normative for the Christian life.

We faced, as most evangelicals do, the challenge of learning the difference between proclaiming truth (God heals) and actually experiencing it. This challenge exists as a result of the worldview most of us have grown up with and been educated to believe. This rational worldview espouses the existence of two discrete, functional realms: a supernatural realm where God and spirit beings operate, and a natural realm that operates according to natural laws. The natural realm, in which we live and operate, functions without much interaction with the supernatural realm. The two realms operate quite independently from each other. In this worldview, the natural realm is run by scientific laws that have no functional, spiritual components.[1]

We have been aided in our understanding of competing worldviews by the writing of Professors Warner, Kraft, and Anderson. They assert that a biblical worldview is one that sees these two realms as being in constant, functional contact with each other. God is a personal, interactive, relational Being, who, as a loving heavenly Father, is concerned for the well-being of His children. The Gospels clearly record this type of interaction in the life of Jesus. He brought the sovereignty, mercy, and grace of God the Father to bear on the human condition. This worldview gives insight into just how the authority of Jesus Christ over the sufferings of His people can be operational today in the church's ministry to the hurting. We believe that all authority is given to Jesus the Christ and that it is absolute and forever. (See Ephesians 1:22.) We believe that because we are seated with Christ we can exercise His authority in ministry to those needing healing. (See Ephesians 2:6.)

The three-level healing model that arose from our new worldview of the interaction between the natural and supernatural is still very much a work in progress. Can any of us comprehend the mystery of God? We know our comprehension is incomplete, however, we have developed a framework that helps us to communicate our degree of understanding of this great work of God in bringing healing to His people.

The first level of this framework identifies our attempt to understand "healing" at a foundational level. Most of us have witnessed the significant healing and change that takes place in a person's life when they encounter the saving grace of Jesus Christ. Healing sometimes occurs relationally, emotionally, spiritually, and physically in the salvation experience. The testimony, given to this author, of a man addicted to cocaine for fifteen years, who was instantly freed of any desire for that drug at the moment of his conversion, stands out as a wonderful reminder of the power inherent in an initial encounter with Jesus Christ.

The human need for belonging, comfort, and love are most often met in the context of Christian community. In our tradition, spiritual growth is nurtured and encouraged through the many opportunities to participate in Bible study, service to others, and worship. Life change occurs as new Christians experience healthy relationships, which are nurtured and guided by biblical teaching in a church. The sanctification process produces changes in behavior, attitudes, and values that are often dramatic. We have witnessed and verified the testimony of those who claim physical and emotional healing took place following baptism or during communion.

However, for most evangelicals, as we integrate new believers into the church body, our focus is on the need to disciple and to teach them. This is because most of us have been influenced by the rational-educational worldview in our approach to ministry to our people. Certainly the process of knowing and experiencing God is Holy Spirit-directed. In order for spiritual growth to occur and the inner man to be transformed, an attitude of obedience and a willingness to confess sin are essential. Our methods, at this first level in the healing process, are ones we are confident of and comfortable with after long experience. These methods include teaching, preaching, counseling, mentoring, discipling, and caring. The results are changed lives that demonstrate growing maturity in Christ, healed relationships, lifestyle changes, and modified worldviews.

Through experience, many people assume that the process, methods, and results described in this first level are sufficient and even perhaps all we can expect. Yet we discerned that many who came to us with spiritual and emotional wounds did not reach the level of healing they desired through the processes of healing they experienced from ministry at level one. For example, more discipleship and mentoring did not seem to help many addicts get free of the bondage of addiction. We learned that our reliance on the things we knew and were most comfortable with in addressing woundedness was misguided, ineffective, and tended to greatly oversimplify a complex issue like addiction.

It became apparent to us that if we were to help the perfectionist, the addict, the individual with a personality disorder, and others with serious wounds, we needed to move beyond techniques based on the rational-educational worldview to a more God-dependent, Holy Spirit-directed approach. Healing needed to occur on a deeper level and we needed to have the knowledge and tools to take the wounded to that level. People with these needs are those we have identified as needing healing at level two. At this level we saw a pronounced need for freedom from spiritual and emotional bondage.

The person who has experimented with occult practices and false religions needs more than a few minutes of prayer and a Bible study to experience freedom and release from the bondage resulting from his exposure to pure idolatry. The person reared by parents who were emotionally distant and detached needs the loving acceptance of her church community, but also needs something more directly focused on the inner woundedness. For these people struggling with what we call level two issues, the combination of the prayer team ministry and counseling is necessary to break the bondage they face. An obedient, humble attitude on the part of the person seeking help is also critically important.

Our prayer teams experienced the functional gifts of the Spirit as they learned to allow the Holy Spirit to use the gifts He had bestowed on them. The gifts of healing, discernment, knowledge, wisdom, and mercy are often evident in the healing process. Confession of sin and renouncing the enemy's footholds are crucial in the process of leading a person to freedom. The methods used at this level include the seven-step model, prayer team ministry, and counseling. The results are often dramatic. We have experienced physical healings, release from spiritual bondage, relational healings, and emotional healings. The resulting increase in faith and trust in a loving, heavenly Father experienced by individuals and their families has been wonderful to observe.

Due to the serious dysfunction of many families, the prevalence of New Age practices, and the general disregard for treating others with consideration and respect, many people need healing at some time in their lives at this deeper level. The evangelical church, in our opinion, has been generally weak at providing this level of ministry. Perhaps this is due to a failure to recognize that many people in our churches need it. However, a look at church history will reveal periods, especially the first three hundred years, when there was a strong emphasis on healing at this level.[2] The needs of our people should compel the modern church to examine our theology, methods, and programs to reestablish the healing ministry of Jesus. (See Frances McNutt's book *The Perfect*

Crime: How the Church Almost Killed the Healing Ministry, for an enlightening discussion of this topic.[3])

While we have developed a degree of comfort and confidence at working in a level two environment, we are still challenged by those who need even deeper levels of healing. Hence, we identified a level three healing that we believe the church is responsible to address. It is at this third level that we encounter the greatest degree of woundedness and pain. The persons needing healing at this deepest level are usually those victimized by severe abuse: ritual, emotional, physical, sexual, or neglect and abandonment. They usually have a long history of seeking help from a variety of mental health professionals. They have often also sought help from countless seminars, books, sermons, prayer meetings, and prayer groups. Most of these people have developed significant distrust of both man and God due to their failure to obtain help in healing their wounds.

Often they have experienced such extreme rejection that anger, self-condemnation, and defensiveness are pronounced personality characteristics. They frequently have difficulty establishing a sense of belonging and joy within the Christian community. The rational-educational approach to ministering to these people does not, in our experience, result in the level of healing needed. The interventions used effectively at level two also do not seem to take us to the depth necessary to see the healing the person so desires and needs. Their concept of God is filled with distortions as a result of their unhealthy and dysfunctional relationships with significant people in their lives. They most often present a distant, disconnected relationship with God characterized by a lack of trust. We will discuss this in detail in chapter 8.

There is, however, in spite of all their rejection and pain, still a desire to seek after God—to establish a healthy, functional relationship with Him and with others. The healing process for these deeply wounded souls is usually a long one. It is both time and resource intensive. A variety of methodologies are needed, including healing prayer, deliverance prayer, persevering prayer, discipleship counseling, mentoring, and lots of acceptance—all delivered with unconditional love. The persistent interaction of caring believers as brothers and sisters in Christ is vital in the healing and restoration process. Many of the people needing this level of healing have suffered much damage from relationships with those who should have been trusted nurturers. It follows that healing must occur in a relational context characterized by unconditional love and acceptance. This connection to the church family is what the Holy Spirit uses to powerfully accomplish healing in the life of the wounded person. The process at this third level is difficult and slow.

The wounded person must be willing to face their fear of rejection and exercise great courage to submit to the ministry of others in their lives. One crucial element those ministering at level three need to address is the individual's need for safety. Developing a safe relationship with another person is necessary if the issues arising from broken and abused trust are to be addressed effectively. For example, one person who came for help was so abused and hurting that it took six months of caring, encouraging, and consistent affirmations of love and respect before she was able to open up and begin to share a part of her painful past.

We often find ourselves asking the question Jesus asked of the invalid at the pool of Bethesda as recorded in John 5:6, "Do you want to get well?" (NIV). The fears and resistance deeply engrained in most deeply wounded people have to be identified and carefully ministered to by the helping teams. Allowing a person to move at his or her own pace is a respectful and considerate thing to do for them. It helps to establish a degree of emotional safety for the person. Although the process is difficult, we can expect to see healing take place because it is not our knowledge, skill, and methodologies that produce healing, but rather the mercy, grace, power, and authority of the Lord Jesus Christ. Through this process we have witnessed healing both emotionally and relationally. We have observed people grow in their relationship with God and become more functional in relating to others. We have seen people experience the freedom that comes when demonic strongholds are broken, allowing them to participate in and benefit from discipleship programs and fellowship with others that the church provides. The process of ministering to level three needs, and the results observed, make us even more conscious of our need to be totally dependent on the Holy Spirit in all areas of our ministry.

The case of Ann (not her real name) is one that helped us to more clearly understand the process God used to bring multilevel healing to a deeply wounded individual. Ann's healing took place over a two-year period and involved the cooperation and contributions of prayer teams and a counselor. Ann first contacted our Pastoral Care Center requesting that a team come to her home to pray for her physical healing. She suffered with a migraine headache for more than a year. She also was diagnosed with fibromyalgia. She had been in bed, unable to care for her husband and four children, and heard that we prayed for the sick to get well.

A prayer team responded to her request and anointed her with oil and prayed for her healing. When healing did not occur, she requested prayer a second time. It was in this second prayer session that one of the team members discerned the presence of demonic activity. At this point she was referred to counseling and began to work with one of our pastoral counseling staff to prepare her to address the work of the enemy in her life. Ann needed to first deal with her own worldview and its resistance to accepting the idea that she could be under attack. In the next few months she continued to experience physical problems but was growing in her relationship with God and understanding He wanted to minister to her body and soul.

She and her counselor spent time analyzing her past experiences, which included involvement with occult practices and false religions as well as the influence of her first husband who, as a Mayan Indian Shaman, practiced his ancient and patently satanic religion. She presented an unusual pattern of needs: emotional, physical, and spiritual. During the process of counseling with her, it was determined that addressing the oppression she experienced was the first priority. The seven-step model was used to confront her spiritual bondage. During the prayer process used in this model (which we will discuss in the next chapter), she was healed of the migraine headache that plagued her for many months. She also experienced a release from the fibromyalgia in the days that followed.

Much work was done to bring her to the point of extending forgiveness to those who had abused her and facilitated her involvement with occult practices and false religions. The combination of prayer intervention and pastoral counseling was the process used powerfully by the Holy Spirit to bring her freedom and healing. Her relationship with God was strengthened and her family witnessed a miracle of God's grace that forever changed their faith. Ann later testified, "I don't think I would be alive today had you not been willing to help me and pray for me."

This case illustrates the need for the church to be the spiritual hospital God designed it to be. Ann sought relief and healing first from the medical profession (she was taking eleven different medications and had consulted with many physicians) with no results. Ann's case involved ministering initially at level two in providing healing prayer. During the prayer process, an accurate spiritual diagnosis of demonic attack was made and the seven-step process was administered. Level three issues were discovered when the degree to which she had been abused by others was revealed. The length of her healing process is also indicative of the complexity of level three issues.

Our experiences with healing and deliverance, as illustrated by Ann's case, led us to believe the church can and should assume its Holy Spirit-empowered role as healer, restorer, and reconciler in the lives of God's people and receive the blessings of being intermediaries to the sovereignty of God. It is this connection with the empowered church family that provides the opportunity for the healing of the whole person. Our prayer is that the Casas healing model will encourage pastors and church leaders to examine their church's position on healing and to take a prayerful, reasoned approach to equipping their people to function as the "spiritual hospital" God designed the church to be.

Chart 3-1
The Casas Healing Model

	LEVEL ONE Knowing and experiencing God	LEVEL TWO Spiritual, emotional, and physical healing	LEVEL THREE Deep Healing
Assumptions	All Christians need healing at this level. The evangelical church is effective at this level.	All Christians need healing at this level to some extent. The evangelical church is generally weak at this level.	Many Christians need healing at this level. The evangelical church seems impotent at this level.
Individual Needs	Salvation, discipleship, community, belonging, acceptance, support, comfort, love, prayer, worship, service	Freedom from spiritual and emotional bondage, physical healing, acceptance, agape love, caring support	Healing of deep, emotional wounds (abuse, neglect, abandonment), deliverance from strongholds, to know God's love, to be accepted, to develop trust, to be loved unconditionally

(continued on next page)

Chart 3-1
The Casas Healing Model

	LEVEL ONE Knowing and experiencing God	LEVEL TWO Spiritual, emotional, and physical healing	LEVEL THREE Deep Healing
Process	Insight oriented, rational-educational, Holy Spirit-directed, obedient application of biblical truth, confession of sin	Holy Spirit-led and empowered, obedient confession, and renouncement of sin	Supernatural work of the Holy Spirit over time, authority of Jesus Christ over suffering and pain, time intensive
Method	Teaching, preaching, counseling, mentoring, discipling, caring	Healing prayer, seven-step prayer, deliverance prayer, discipleship, counseling, flow of spiritual giftings	Healing prayer, deliverance prayer, persevering prayer
Results	Spiritual growth, relational healing, worldview modified, lifestyle values change, comfort, support, reconciliation with God and others, experiencing God's love	Spiritual and emotional freedom, deliverance, relational healing, physical healing, increase in faith, spiritual growth enhanced, experiencing God's love	Healing of emotions, deliverance from demonic, relational healing, trust of God and others

CHAPTER 4

HELPING THOSE IN SPIRITUAL BONDAGE

The Casas healing model assumes there are three fundamental diagnostic categories that must be evaluated in the process of preparing to help hurting people. A client's suffering could have medical causes that would therefore require appropriate medical evaluation and treatment. We also know that psychological factors can result in a number of troubling and painful symptoms and may be the underlying cause of the problem brought to us. Finally our experience and observation have taught us that demonic oppression can produce many of the same symptoms often ascribed to medical or psychological causes. While the diagnostic process is often not an easy one, it has been our experience that including all three categories as "possible" contributors to the issue before us is a balanced, thorough, and effective approach to identifying the cause or causes of the suffering being experienced.

Betty came to us for help after being referred to us by some concerned friends who observed that her depression did not respond to either medical treatment (anti-depressants) or psychological treatment (counseling). She had been taking medication for about two months and had been working with a Christian psychologist for over six weeks. She reported no change for the better in her condition. It was suggested by her friends that she consider a third possible cause for her depression—demonic oppression. Like most of us would be, she was reluctant to even consider such a possibility, but being desperate to get some relief, she called us for an appointment. Because she already considered and sought medical and psychological treatment we were able to move directly to investigating the possibility of demonic attack.

We use the Non-Christian Spiritual Experience Inventory and the Have You Ever... questions (see Appendices A and B) to help us and the client identify possible "open doors" through which the enemy may have gained access to their lives. The Indicators of Demonic Oppression/Attack Check List (Appendix C) is also helpful in identifying symptoms that may be the result of demonic attack. It is crucial to the diagnostic process that experiences with the occult, cults, false religions, and generational involvement with these idolatrous practices be identified. Through this interview process, we determined that Betty's depression was probably due to demonic attack. As part of the initial interview, we also included teaching on spiritual warfare as a means of helping to prepare her to deal with the oppression. We assembled a prayer team, which included those with the spiritual gift of discernment.

In our prayer session, Betty revealed to us that she had gone to a "faith healer" to seek relief from another physical problem. The "healer," who was from Africa, laid hands on her and prayed over her in a language she did not understand. Betty assumed, as many naively do, that everything supernatural is from God. Using the spiritual gift of discernment, we discovered that a demonic spirit had been assigned or transferred to her during this laying on of hands ceremony. When she took her position in Christ and exercised His authority over the work of the enemy by confessing her sin (placing her faith in someone other that God), and rebuked the devil's presence, the oppression was lifted instantly. She was freed from the spirit of depression, and to our knowledge never suffered from any relapse.

This case was our first experience in dealing with the demonic as the direct cause of depression. It established our belief in and practice of the validity of the diagnostic triad—considering the possibility of demonic attack along with possible physical and psychological causes for symptoms. Because of our biblical worldview, we determined that consideration of the work of the enemy as a possible cause of the suffering of the saints is always an appropriate and responsible course of action. We have worked with other cases since Betty's in which demonic influence was "transferred" during the laying on of hands by individuals like psychic healers and channelers who were tapping into spiritual forces other than the Holy Spirit.

We were aided in our learning about how the enemy attacks Christians by the contributions of Dr. Mark Bubeck, as well as the writings of Tom White, and Dr. Neil Anderson, both of whom led conferences at our church on the subject of spiritual warfare. Dr. Charles Kraft, Dr. Timothy Warner, Dr. C. Fred Dickinson, and Dr. Frances McNutt were also influential in the formation of our worldview and our approach to helping the oppressed.

Our goal is to maintain a balanced, reasoned approach to this ministry. We define a balanced position as one that acknowledges, as Jesus did, Satan's existence, power, and influence. (See Roger Barrier's sermon notes in Appendix D.)[1] Jesus refers to Satan as the evil genius, the prince—ruler of this world. (See John 14:30.) Such a position must include a clear understanding of the victory of the cross and the absolute authority of the risen Christ over all other powers and authorities. (See Colossians 2:15; Ephesians 1:21.)

Though God is sovereign, we recognize that there is a spiritual conflict taking place as a result of God giving freedom of choice to beings in both the natural and supernatural realms. When we confront the fallout of this battle in the life of a believer, we are bringing the authority of Jesus Christ and the Holy Spirit to participate in the eviction of the demonic powers, who are merely usurpers, deceivers, and liars. (See John 14:12; 20:21; Ephesians 6:11–12.) We operate from the position that Satan is a defeated foe who has been given a certain amount of freedom to operate under the ultimate sovereignty of God. We believe it is our mission as the church empowered to reveal (Eph. 3:10–11), to expose (Eph. 5:11), to resist (2 Cor. 10:3), and to overcome the work of the devil. (See 1 John 2:14.)

Given our scriptural understanding and our years of validation and confirming experience, we believe that Christians can be oppressed by the enemy. It is our firm conviction that as believers in Jesus Christ, we cannot be possessed by demonic powers. However, as mentioned in chapter 2, the translation "demon possessed" fails to convey the concept of Scripture that would be .more accurately communicated by the word *demonized* or simply *to have a demon*. The concept of "possessed" greatly overstates the influence and power of the demonic. While a Christian can be attacked and oppressed, he cannot be possessed or owned by the enemy.

As we understand it, when a person accepts Christ, he is in essence owned and occupied by the Holy Spirit, and there is therefore no room for the devil to occupy the same life. There is however a capacity to sin on the part of the believer. Sin then is the "port of entry" by which the enemy can gain access. It is tragic in our view for Christians to throw the baby out with the bath water and assert that since Christians cannot be possessed that a ministry to Christians with demonic interference in their lives is an oxymoron. Dr. Kraft addresses this issue most thoroughly in his book, *Confronting Powerless Christianity.*

Our twenty years of experience in helping Christians obtain freedom from demonic attack stands in stark opposition to those who would ignore the reality of the spiritual battle around us and hide behind misguided, misinformed reasoning and faulty biblical interpretation. We have chosen to confront the reality of the spirit realm and to try and understand how Christians can come under attack from the enemy. The reality of life is that Christians can be attacked (oppressed) through sin; either through their own sinful choices or by sin committed against him by others. It is somehow accepted by most evangelicals that a person can bring into their Christian life sinful patterns, thoughts, behaviors, and values, but not demonic influence. We have helped hundreds of Christians experience freedom from demonic attacks by recognizing the difference between "possession" and "oppression."

Early in our experience, we realized that the demonic must have some ground from which to ensure their accessibility to harass and attack Christians. We often use the metaphor of South Pacific island warfare during World War II as an illustration of what may be taking place in the spirit realm. As U.S. forces took ownership of an island and established their occupation, they still had to deal with harassing fire from enemy snipers who remained in fortified pockets of resistance. As our soldiers were building airfields and establishing a base of operations, the enemy still posed a threat to them. Even though the enemy no longer owned the island, their previous occupancy left them in a position of strength to continue to fight against our men. When our soldiers came under attack from the pockets of enemy forces, they stopped what they were doing and engaged the enemy and stopped his attack. We witness the same kind of battle taking place in a Christian's life as pockets of enemy resistance are identified and eliminated so that freedom can be experienced.

A review of the work of the authors mentioned above reveals six major "points of entry" and "pockets of resistance" the demonic exploits in gaining access to bring oppression into the lives of believers.

Occultic Sin

Involvement with the occult and New Age beliefs and practices as well as false religions is idolatry in its purest form. (See Leviticus 20:27; Deuteronomy 18:19.) We have sought to help our people understand what constitutes idolatry by adopting a definition to help guide them. Idolatry is the replacement of God in the heart or mind of an individual by any material object, relationship, fleshly desire, false religion, or occultic practice. (See our Policy Statement on Idolatry in Appendix E.) We use the Non-Christian Spiritual Experience Inventory, originally designed by Dr. Neil Anderson and adapted by our staff, to help people identify the specifics of idolatry in their lives. This helpful resource (see Appendix A) has been organized by degree of severity so as to help us identify possible corresponding degrees of oppression. Many have opened themselves up to demonic influence innocently and out of ignorance. As a result, they are unaware of the dangerous influence of their choices. However innocence and ignorance are not any protection against the influence of the demonic. There are also some who have purposefully sought after these experiences, practices, and beliefs. Their bondage to the "ruler of this world" can be more severe than that of those who innocently opened themselves to attack. Many people come to our church having been under the influence of false teaching and have experiences in cults. Some come to us wounded and fearful from their involvement in legalistic and spiritually abusive churches. It might surprise many pastors to learn of the extent to which members of their congregation have been or are currently involved in many of these idolatrous activities and damaging belief systems. It is our experience that many people in our congregations are in bondage and need help in getting free.

Habitual Sin

The habitual practice of sin allows the devil to establish a foothold in a person's life. This principle is clearly taught in Ephesians 4:26–27. Paul used the common experience of not dealing with anger and the bitterness that results as his example. We have experienced and observed this process over and over in the lives of believers. As a person repeatedly chooses to commit the same sin over and over, demonic forces gradually acquire influence and control over that particular area of the person's life. For example, the choice to give in to lust and view pornography often leads to an addiction to pornography. Likewise the repetitive choice to seek relief from emotional pain by overeating frequently leads to a food addiction. If this repetitive pattern goes on long enough, the person may lose control to the point that the sinful pattern becomes more an expression of the demonic influence than of the person's own personality. The "usurper" gains access through the open door of rebellion and disobedience as a person refuses over time to deal with a sinful pattern or practice. Sexual sin patterns and practices is one area that is a source of stronghold and bondage for many. It is important for the church to not only teach and preach about biblical standards for sexuality, but also to address the bondage many struggle with as the result of habitual sin patterns.

Generational Sin

The sins of great grandparents, grandparents, and parents can, in a spiritual sense, influence and impact one's life. (See Exodus 20:5; Leviticus 26:39–40; Numbers 14:17–18; Jeremiah 23:18; John 9:2–3.) It is widely accepted by those in spiritual warfare ministries that spiritual doorways can be opened by the unconfessed sins of our ancestors.[2] For example, we have witnessed this spiritual principle in operation in the lives of those whose ancestors practiced some form of idolatry. The most commonly encountered practices include witchcraft, spiritualism, freemasonry, sorcery, and New Age teachings. The influence of these idolatrous practices seem to manifest symptomatically in subsequent generations with a lack of interest in Bible study and worship; unbelief in the miracles of Jesus and His authority over the works of the devil; being drawn toward New Age and occultic practices and teachings; and a tendency toward a lack of spiritual security, which leads to persistent spiritual searching and questioning. It seems that when generational sin is operating, the individual is unable to prosper and grow spiritually. While there are certainly environmental and genetic factors at play in explaining the existence of patterns of behavior in families from generation to generation, they do not mitigate the possibility there could also be spiritual forces at work as well. The most exhaustive work on this subject was done by Dr. C. Fred Dickinson in his book *Demon Possession and the Christian.*

Sins of Others

While it may offend our sense of justice, the reality is that sins committed against us by another leave emotional wounds that in turn may be exploited by the enemy and his demonic hosts. For example, severe abuse of a child will often result in the abused person having a stronghold of bondage to fear, resentment, self-destruction, or addiction, to name of few of the possibilities.

Peter (1 Pet. 5:8) describes Satan as a roaring lion prowling around looking for those he can devour. In the wild, a lion will go after the weak, the young, the old, and the wounded as its first choice of prey. Time and time again we have seen the emotionally wounded being attacked and oppressed by the enemy. The good news is that when Jesus heals the wounds, the "ground" is taken away from the squatters and usurper, and they leave. To help understand how this principle works, it may be helpful to think of demonic forces being attracted to emotional and spiritual woundedness just as flies are to open physical wounds. In both the natural and supernatural realms, healing is the key to eliminating the presence of these pests. It should also be mentioned here that emotional trauma experienced as the result of accidents, just as trauma produced by the sin of others like murder, rape, torture, and terrorism, can be and often is exploited by the demonic.

Direct Attack by Occultists

Paul and Barnabas's experiences with the false prophet and sorcerer Elymas, as recorded in Acts 13:10, and Paul and Silas's encounter with the demon-possessed slave girl in Acts 16:16–19, give us a biblical record of how the enemy uses others to attack God's people. We were made aware of this reality when one of our prison ministry workers had an encounter with an inmate. When the inmate found out what church the visitor was from, he stated: "Oh, I used to pray against your church when I was in my coven." When our astonished worker asked, "What were you praying for?" the inmate responded: "We were praying that your ministers would have affairs and their marriages would fail." We discovered that there were actually four other churches being prayed against, along with Casas. In retrospect, we could see that these attacks were felt to some degree by all five churches. There were ministers who lost their jobs due to adultery and divorce, and one church experienced the accidental death of their pastor. While each reader will have to assess the correlation between these events and the prayers of the enemy for themselves, it would be naïve of us to ignore the reality that the enemy targets Christians and their churches.

Strategic Ministry

Anyone who assumes a position of leadership and responsibility in the kingdom becomes a target for the enemy's attacks and oppression. Paul's direct confrontation with the work of the enemy on the streets of Ephesus and the resulting satanic counterattack in the form of a riot (Acts 19:23), illustrate the fact that strategic warfare against enemy strongholds can result in specific, targeted counterattacks against the soldiers of the King.

We have helped many a fallen pastor and wounded missionary who, in hindsight, realized that they had been targeted for attack and destruction. Often the means for the enemy to gain access to them was through an unconfessed sin and/or unhealed emotional woundedness of the individual that had never been addressed prayerfully and therapeutically. In the last chapter, we shared Ann's story. Ann's headaches began when her daughter went on a youth missions trip to Mexico to work in the village where her father, Ann's ex-husband, was the shaman. As in this case, such attacks are often frontal, blatant, and direct, springing from hostile opposition from people who try to prevent the work of God from progressing. As a result of being the victim of the enemy's attacks on the mission field, former missionaries like C. Peter and Doris Wagner, Timothy Warner, Charles Kraft, and Ed Murphy all returned to teach seminary courses on spiritual warfare in order to better equip those entering fields of strategic ministry for the spiritual battles they would encounter.

As we gained an understanding of how believers can be attacked and oppressed, it helped us to identify the nature of the strongholds and bondages and devise a strategy to help set these believers free. Our strategy involves a thorough evaluation and assessment using the Non-Christian Spiritual Experiences Inventory, the Have You Ever... questions, and the Indicators of Demonic Oppression/Attack. As previously indicated, we rely on the counseling relationship to provide a context in which to explore the possibility of the enemy's work as a cause of problems in a person's life. The building of trust between the helper and the help-ee is invaluable in providing the freedom and confidence necessary to uncover areas of bondage.

For our framework, we selected the Freedom in Christ model developed by Dr. Neil Anderson, former professor of practical theology at Talbot Seminary. We did so with the awareness that others use and find effective the power encounter model (confronting the demonic directly and by name) in their deliverance ministries. For example, Dr. Charles Kraft uses this approach in dealing with those in spiritual bondage.[3] We chose Dr. Anderson's model as our primary approach to helping the oppressed deal with the enemy's work in their lives because of its structure, biblical foundation, easy-to-use format, and because it places the responsibility for confessing sin and renouncing the devil on the individual. The prayer process using the seven steps is something we do *with* the person, not *for* or *to* the person. This model fits our understanding and practice of Christian discipleship as well as our counseling philosophy, which is centered in client responsibility. We have used it since 1994 and found it to be a useful and practical tool. Research has been conducted on the effectiveness of this model yielding positive results.[4]

A brief description of the seven-step prayer model is included in Appendix F. Procedurally, we follow the general guidelines as recommended by the Freedom in Christ ministry. The client is asked to read Dr. Anderson's *Victory Over Darkness* and *The Bondage Breaker*. He or she is also required to complete a comprehensive questionnaire. When the individual has demonstrated a commitment to the process and has completed all of the preparation assigned, then a prayer team is assembled and a time scheduled for the session. We have discovered it is important to use same-sex prayer teams and to schedule adequate time to allow for the completion of the entire session at one time. The average time for most men is three to five hours, while most women take five to eight hours to complete the process.

No one is required to go through the process. It is always the individual's decision predicated on his or her willingness to be totally honest and humble before the team working with them. The team consists of trained persons—one facilitator and one prayer partner. They lead the person using the provided *Steps to Freedom in Christ* workbook, through the seven prayers.[5] We have encountered cases in which the prerequisite preparation was suspended due to the severity of the bondage. The guiding principle is that the individual must be sincere in submitting to God and willing to be obedient to the admonition in James 5:16, to "confess your sins to each another." There are some who cannot read the books due to learning disabilities or because their English is not good enough to comprehend what they are reading. In these cases we go ahead and lead them through the steps of the process, explaining, coaching, and teaching as we do.

We like this model and have found it universally helpful and effective. It is based on two biblically accurate and spiritually powerful concepts: confession of sin and renunciation of the devil. (See James 5:16; 2 Corinthians 4:2.) The confession of sin to one another is powerful in breaking self-condemnation and shame. It requires a level of humility that God uses to bring healing and freedom. Renunciation addresses the extent to which the enemy has gained access to the person's life and has established footholds. Another benefit of Anderson's model is that it provides structure and direction on how to assume authority over the demonic, and practical steps for how to get free and stay free after the initial prayer session has been completed. The *Steps to Freedom in Christ* workbook is given to the individual to take home and use whenever the need for maintaining freedom arises. The section in the workbook titled "In Christ" is a powerful resource for helping the individual maintain a biblically sound self-image and overcome the lies that they have believed about themselves, others, and God.[6]

It has been our experience that when areas of bondage are released, the individual is free to respond to and participate in the insight-cognitive oriented process of internalizing biblical truth and experiencing changes in attitude, behavior, values, and worldview. We believe that, to some extent, all of us have some issues of bondage that need liberating. We all have "closets full of junk" in our spiritual houses that need a good cleaning out. The seven-step model provides one way to accomplish the cleaning task. It should not and is not purported to be the answer to every need or "the magic bullet" for all hurting people. It is a tool that has been used powerfully by the Holy Spirit to heal and restore many.

The use of this model is so well integrated into the flow of the helping process at Casas that it has become a functional part of how we help hurting people. For example, we have found that when couples who are having marital difficulty are led through the seven steps individually, it results in reducing the number of counseling sessions that normally would be needed and increasing the effectiveness of the sessions that are completed. In some cases the change in the individuals have been so dramatic that marital counseling has not even been necessary. This is not, however, the only prayer model we use. Prayer for inner healing is often used because it is appropriate to the situation due to the level of healing required. It is important to not get too focused on the process or the model used. Healing and freeing from bondage is the work of the Holy Spirit and is not dependent on the approach or model one uses or on the experience or skill of the helper. It has been our experience that being flexible, open to the leading of the Holy Spirit, and willing to continue to learn about ministry to the oppressed, are important for maintaining a vibrant and effective ministry.

CHAPTER 5

HELPING DIFFICULT PEOPLE

Pastors and lay leaders often encounter individuals who demand more time than others, present a plethora of needs they expect the church to meet, and don't seem to make much progress in taking responsibility for their own health and well-being in spite of the efforts of many caring helpers. It is the purpose of this chapter to identify classifications of individuals who are difficult to work with at best and perhaps at worst, are people we cannot help to make significant changes in their lives. Ministers are challenged by these "difficult people" in that their desire to be compassionate and caring is hooked by the skillful presentation of needs and corresponding expectations for the allocation of time and resources to meet those needs.

Difficult people usually present a common set of characteristics, which help us to identify them early in the process of deciding how to meet their needs and demands.

- ▸ Lack of a teachable spirit
- ▸ Disregard for the rights and needs of others
- ▸ Inability to learn from negative and punishing experiences
- ▸ Pervasive relational conflict
- ▸ Consuming selfishness
- ▸ Crisis orientation to life
- ▸ Failure to accept responsibility for their own behavior
- ▸ Demonstrate a shallow, distorted, and immature relationship with God
- ▸ Inability to view themselves objectively

The assumption being presented here is often difficult for caring pastors and lay leaders to accept: there are people we don't seem to be able to help. That is to say that, despite the best efforts of those who try to help, we fail to see significant change in attitude, behavior, and in the ability to relate in healthy ways to God and others. The mental health community labels individuals with these characteristics as having a personality disorder. A personality disorder is defined as pervasive, unchanging, and maladaptive as it is manifested in a personality. An individual with a personality disorder displays a distorted way of living and managing their affairs and relationships, and has a persistent, unchanging, and incorrect way of perceiving, thinking, and relating to the world around them.

These individuals do not see themselves as the major contributing cause of their own difficulties. They leave trails of disturbed, interpersonal relationships by behavior that is persistent, long-term, and highly resistant to change. They do not see their maladaptive behavior as unusual. They consistently fail to see themselves as others do.[1] They therefore seldom seek professional help, and when they do, it is usually a result of pressure from a spouse, family member, employer, or the legal system. They lack the personal insight and motivation for change and therefore are usually resistant to the pastor's referral to a mental health professional. A person with a personality disorder will often perceive the church in the same way they do others in their lives. They expect the church to meet their needs on demand.

Personality disorders differ from psychotic conditions in that disorders do not have delusions or hallucinations associated with them. While a psychotic person may believe the police are watching him and distracting him from doing his work, a personality disordered person would see his poor job performance as his employer's or a coworker's fault. A person with a personality disorder usually does not experience anxiety about his or her behavior, because they do not see it as unusual or inappropriate. A person suffering from claustrophobia, for example, knows that the anxiety they experience in riding on an elevator is not normal, and usually will seek help to alleviate his suffering. A person with a personality disorder, however, tends to see the conflict and pain in their marriage as their spouse's fault and expects them to resolve it. Personality disorders also differ from mood disorders such as depression and anxiety, and they are different from bipolar disorder with mood swings from mania to depression.

The question that is frequently asked when discussing personality disorders is: How do they develop? It is generally accepted that they are formed during childhood from experiences of abandonment, abuse, and neglect. The traits produced by the individual's response to these experiences are usually set by late adolescence. As a child experiences the trauma of abuse, neglect, or abandonment, they formed conclusions about self, God, and others that seem to explain why the painful experience occurred. The childish mind is not capable of reaching correct assessments about their self-worth, competence, and place of belonging. Personality disordered people are governed by beliefs that are not true. Because they are unable to examine themselves objectively, they tend to continue believing and accepting their distortions of reality as truth.

Studies on the prevalence of personality disorders in the general population suggest that 5 to 15 percent of the U.S. population have some kind of personality disorder.[2] Four personality disorders have been selected for detailed examination in this chapter, because in our experience they are the most common encountered in church ministry. A brief description of the other six, as identified in the DSM-IV, are provided at the end of this chapter.

The Histrionic Personality Disorder

This is most often found in females who are in need of attention and affection to accommodate their poor self-esteem and fragile self-confidence (see chart 5-1 for diagnostic criteria). Histrionics are, at first meeting, outgoing, friendly, and talkative. However more extended contact with them reveals the defining characteristics of their disorder. They have an all-consuming need to be noticed and to be given special attention. They tend to be lively, colorful, and dramatic, but their thinking is superficial and their emotions shallow. They are creative, imaginative, and often have an artistic flair for the dramatic. They may actively seek expressions of admiration and praise from others through dramatic, attention-seeking behaviors. They will often dress seductively to get male attention, especially the attention of prominent men like pastors.

They will demonstrate a low tolerance for frustration or delay. For example, they frequently get angry with the pastor's secretary, who may have difficulty meeting the demand for appointments. They will often be drawn to the "up front" ministries of the church. Worship teams, choirs, drama, and dance groups are among those most frequently chosen by this personality type. When histrionics have specific talents, like vocal ability, they are often successful in getting the attention they need and desire from the congregation. The popularity they therefore engender in the church keeps pastors on their toes in trying to deal with their unhealthy behavior without seeming to communicate to the individual or to the church that they are uncaring or inconsiderate.

It has been our experience that histrionics draw attention to themselves by inappropriate behaviors. On more than one occasion, women we would recognize as having histrionic traits have been asked to go home and change into less-revealing clothing before attending choir practice or singing on Sunday morning. These women seem to be uninterested in Bible study and fail to learn much from sermons, perhaps because of their shallow thinking and processing abilities. It is important to realize that they are at church and involved, not because they want to grow spiritually, but rather because it is a place they can get the social attention and personal recognition they are driven to obtain.

One of the ways they get these needs met is to be seen talking to the leadership and getting to know them personally. Counseling appointments with pastors are important, because they focus attention exclusively on the individual. The status gain in the eyes of others because of a "relationship" with the pastor is highly motivating and reinforcing for this personality disorder. Histrionics are often attractive, seductive, entertaining, and fun to be around. They therefore pose a threat to the naïve pastor who is not fully aware of his own needs for attention and flattery. We all know of those in ministry who have allowed themselves to become emotionally and sometimes sexually involved with these charming and exciting women. In Proverbs 11:22, it warns us of such a personality type: "A beautiful woman who lacks discretion is like a gold ring in a pig's snout."

It is important for us to have a strategy in mind to deal with personality disorders. Setting reasonable boundaries is basic.

1. *Set specific limits on the amount of time to be spent in ministry to these individuals.* Limit counseling sessions to the first one requested. After that, refer the person with the histrionic disorder to a female Christian counselor. Pastors should limit the amount of time they spend talking to such a woman in the aisle of the church after services and in other informal settings. Even after they are referred to others for help that likely will not eliminate their continued requests for the pastor's personal intervention and help. It is important to remember that they are asking for attention and not taking responsibility for their own issues. When their requests are granted, it only reinforces their belief that they need and deserve the attention given.

2. *Deal with inappropriate behaviors by setting and maintaining healthy boundaries.* For example, coming to choir practice in short shorts and a tank top is not acceptable. Phone calls to the pastor's home in evenings and on days off are also

inappropriate and should not be rewarded with success. Pastors would be well advised to use their spouse and secretary to prevent direct access both at home and at the office.

3. *Accept the reality that like other personality disordered individuals, the histrionic will not be able to function in a healthy way as she relates to others in your congregation.* For example, allowing one person to dominate a prayer meeting with her own issues every week cannot be tolerated. We have a duty of care to protect our congregations from disturbing behaviors that interfere with worship and service. It has been our experience that when boundaries are set and enforced, the histrionic will go elsewhere to seek the "special treatment" they believe they deserve. The next church or organization they choose will probably hear a negative critique about how they were treated by the pastor and church they last attended.

The Dependent Personality Disorder

This disorder, also called the professional client syndrome, is also difficult to deal with because what looks on the surface like healthy behavior is actually quite unhealthy. (See chart 5-2 for diagnostic criteria.) Submission to authority is healthy, but dependence and compliance out of a need to be taken care of is not healthy. The dependent personality is driven relationally by a desire to be secure and safe because of a deeply held perception that they are unable to care for themselves. This person sees himself as inadequate and insecure, lacking in self-confidence. He therefore needs to live off the strengths of others. These people are drawn to strong leaders who will help them deal with the complexities of life. Making decisions is difficult for them due to a lack of self-confidence; therefore they tend to attach themselves to stronger people who can then make their decisions for them.

These people are willing to go to excessive lengths to gain approval and personal validation. They might volunteer for a number of jobs in the church, including the most undesirable, in order to gain approval. They see aloneness as their own personal hell and must be attached to another person to avoid the pervasive fear that they can't take care of themselves. We have experienced this in the case of an older woman mentoring a younger one. We never saw one without the other. The time they spent together was exclusive and excessive. The dependent person was allowing the mentor to make her decisions for her and to support her in all aspects of her life. The church accepted this mentoring arrangement as appropriate under the biblical model of guidance from older women helping younger women. The mentor label provided an effective camouflage covering for an unhealthy relationship. The mentor thought she was helping this needy person without realizing she was in fact enabling her to avoid taking responsibility for her own life.

The dependent person has in essence displaced God in their lives with relationships that provide the security they believe they need to survive. This unhealthy and idolatrous pattern inhibits their spiritual development. We as the church do not want to be in a position of enabling unhealthy behavior that actually works counter to our efforts to encourage spiritual growth. We can help the dependent person by helping them recognize that they are in the right place. The church can provide healthy relationships as a model for relational maturation and dependence on God.

We can acquire basic knowledge and understanding of how this personality disorder manifests itself and identify healthy boundaries for all involved. We can encourage and maybe even require counseling and prayer team intervention. We can provide educational and support group opportunities to assist and enhance the healing process. We can hold the individual accountable to cooperate with a strategy that moves them toward healing and wholeness. We can confront their mistaken belief that they need someone to be available to help them at all times. We can help them to see their own distortions of who God is by discipleship, counseling, and mentoring.

This process of helping must be tempered by the reality that a pattern of dependence is pervasive and long standing. We must take into account the fact that the person will be very subservient in order to maintain goodwill with those who try to help. This subservience will often look like cooperation and commitment to change when in fact it is just the opposite. Like all personality disorders, these dependent personalities are difficult to work with because of their extreme neediness. The dependent personality presents a particular challenge in that their behavior will not be as extreme or disruptive to the congregation as are many of the others. A helping strategy must take into account that their worldview is dominated by the belief that they are helpless and weak. Proverbs 16:20 (NIV) is an appropriate verse to pray on behalf of this personality: "Whoever gives heed to instruction prospers, and blessed is he who trusts in the LORD." A strategy for working with these individuals should include the following:

1. *Seek to put the responsibility for decision making on the individual.* Help them to identify options, but insist that they make the choice themself. (This

process is strikingly similar to parenting a three-year-old child!)

2. *Avoid rescuing them from a crisis.* Work to help them assume responsibility for dealing with a particular issue as you coach them through it.

3. *Place limits on the amount of time they get from you; both on the phone and in person.*

4. *Model that it is appropriate and normal to disagree and still be friends.*

5. *Help them to achieve success by encouraging them to complete a task on their own.*

6. *Be assertive in confronting their dependent patterns of behavior and their fears of being left alone.*

7. *Pray for wisdom and pray for and with them to confront their fears.*

The Antisocial Personality Disorder

A person with this disorder, a sociopath, is one that is almost impossible to effectively deal with. (See chart 5-3 for diagnostic criteria.) A person with this disorder is usually male and is in constant conflict with society and with individuals. They exhibit pervasive patterns of rebellious, irresponsible, manipulative, controlling, and often violent, aggressive behavior. They believe that their needs must be met, and they feel justified in using whatever means are necessary to insure that they are met. The anti-social personality disordered individual feels no guilt or remorse for actions that might be harmful to others. In church work we encounter this personality usually in the context of marital and family conflict. If they are single, they will often attend singles functions for the purpose of connecting with romantic interests.

These people often have had multiple marriages and have not accepted responsibility for the support of dependent children. They are often candidates for church discipline because of the disruption their behavior causes. It is also possible they may seek out a pastor's support by appearing depressed or anxious and even penitent in response to an encounter with the law or a failed marriage. Their agenda in these circumstances is to enlist the aid of the pastor to make themselves more credible in the eyes of a judge, probation officer, attorney, or family member. The pastor is a means to an end for this personality. Genuine repentance is usually quite rare for these individuals.

Churches have also encountered this personality in doing business with the community. It is our experience that they are often found in the skilled trades and likely to be in conflict with the church over a contractual dispute or job-related issue. This disorder falls into two subgroups. The first is the "con-man," who is charming, usually physically attractive to women, intelligent, and possesses good verbal and manipulative skills. This personality is one we have encountered most frequently in our singles and benevolence ministries. Underneath the charming façade lies a hidden agenda—an agenda that says, "I will get what I want." This personality is also the one that is behind the financial frauds that have victimized many churches and Christian organizations. The second is the more antagonistic, aggressive, and often violent of the two. This individual shows no regard for the rights of others, has no compassion for them, and shows no remorse or regret for any harm he may have done. Our prisons are populated by men with this disorder.

Both of these subgroups harbor a great deal of hostility, but they differ in the way it is expressed. The charmer masks hostility toward women by being kind, gracious, and even spiritual, until he gets what he wants from them. We have observed on many occasions the charmer attending a singles class and quickly establishing a dating relationship that leads, in a short time, to marriage. The relationship soon encounters rough waters as his real personality emerges and the wife sadly reports, "This isn't the man I married." The level of the hostility experienced by the wife is in sharp contrast to the way she was treated during courtship. Antisocial personality disordered persons are most often financially irresponsible, sexually manipulative, and promiscuous.

They are skilled at intimidation and deception. They trust no one, usually because they could never trust their parents who were abusive and neglectful. The grid through which they see their world is distorted by extreme hostility and distrust. These are pervasive patterns deeply engrained and, in the majority of cases, do not change. For those of us who encounter them in church ministry, their behavior is not just troubling, it is often dangerous and injurious to the body of Christ. It is important to recognize that these people do not gain insight from the teaching of biblical truth about how people are to be treated. Their worldview is characterized by grave distortions. For example, they consistently believe they are right and the other person is wrong. They believe their needs always take precedence over the rights of others and that people are to be used to meet their needs.

If undesirable consequences do occur as a result of their behavior, they tend to blame others and act as if it doesn't matter to them. They seem to be incapable of accepting responsibility for their own behavior and usually never apologize for any hurtful action. Because of the nature of this disorder, it is incumbent upon church leadership to protect the congregation from being exploited and harmed. In order to be effective in our duty of care we must have a strategy in place that includes the following:

1. *Recognize that a person with this disorder is highly skilled and manipulative at getting what he wants from people.* They are users and takers, not givers. They will use religion and spirituality as means of gaining the esteem of others to accomplish their personal goals rather than to develop a relationship with God.

2. *Setting of firm limits is essential in order to maintain control.* We have learned to confront the behavior of these individuals with firmness by putting in writing the rules they must follow in order to remain in our church. When confronted in this way almost all choose to leave and go where they can work their agenda unhindered. It is important for a pastor to alert the new pastor if he learns they have gone to another church. Some may choose a more aggressive and hostile response when asked to obey the rules or leave. In some cases their threats must be met with appropriate legal action. We have exercised our legal rights to insure protection for our staff and church. Police protection has been obtained for Sunday services on more than one occasion. It is usually the case, although it is not a certainty, that

when confronted with power, they will retreat and seek another place where they are freer to operate.

3. *Accept the fact that this personality type can't be helped and focus resources on helping and supporting those hurt by him.* In most cases, efforts to help individuals with this personality disorder end in failure and frustration. Referral to a mental health professional is usually futile unless it is backed up by a court order. They resist seeking help because of their deeply held belief that others are to blame. The mental health professions agree that the prognosis for a "cure" or even a partial cure is poor.[3] The Book of Proverbs identifies this personality disorder with amazing clarity: "Mockers are proud and haughty; they act with boundless arrogance" (Prov. 21:24). "A single rebuke does more for a person of understanding than a hundred lashes on the back of a fool" (Prov. 17:10). "Though his speech is charming, do not believe him, for seven abominations fill his heart" (Prov. 26:25, NIV).

The Borderline Personality Disorder

This disorder occurs three times more often in women than men, and affects 2 to 3 percent of the U.S. population.[4] The term *borderline* was originally used to indicate the person was on the edge of psychosis. While under stress, the borderline personality disordered person may manifest some symptoms of psychosis, but they seldom become psychotic. They are however deeply troubled people who characteristically are unable to sustain healthy relationships. They tend to be rigid in their thinking and have little tolerance for the inconsistencies and weaknesses of others. They are demanding and get anxious and angry when their needs are not addressed in a timely manner. (See chart 5-4 for diagnostic criteria.) They often present themselves well at first contact. They might do well in a job or ministry interview but don't perform well once they are hired or selected.

These people are difficult in a church context because of their demanding nature. The church never measures up to their expectations, resulting in a constant level of frustration with the leadership. They are often paranoid and misread others as attacking them personally. Their mood swings are unpredictable and without reason. When they seek the help of a pastor or counselor, they may disclose a long history of treatment for bipolar disorder with poor long-term success. They often have tried a variety of medications with only short-term improvement followed by a return of symptoms. Rarely will they identify their problems as resulting from a personality disorder, but will instead complain about uncontrollable changes in mood. They fear being alone, yet because of their own faulty thinking and emotional volatility, they drive others away and end up alone. They send mixed messages like, "I love you, but I don't like you," and, "Go away; don't leave me."

Borderlines trust no one and tend to interpret the behavior of others in ways that validates their distrust. For example, not being called on to read a passage of Scripture in a Bible study group can be interpreted as, "The leader doesn't really like me and is a poor leader." They tend to disrupt group dynamics by their critical attitude of others in the group. They see themselves as right and others as wrong in most situations of conflict. Their recollection and interpretation of what someone said and did is, in their view, always the correct one. Their lives are characterized by constant relational conflict and tension. They usually have an employment history of many job changes and are frequently out of work. They tend to expect the church to provide financial assistance during these times of unemployment, which is seen as the result of poor management on the part of their previous employer.

They also tend to have a history of moving from church to church for the same reasons. Pastors often go from hero status to jerk status quickly in the minds of these whose expectations are so unrealistic. They tend to be legalistic and rigid in their interpretation of Scripture due to their inability to deal in a healthy way with theological gray areas. Borderlines are usually above average in intelligence, and have good verbal skills. They are, therefore, very effective in getting what they want from others. They pose a challenge to churches because their needs know no bounds. They seem to live from one crisis to another, and do not gain lasting benefit from the financial, emotional, or spiritual help that is provided. The following suggestions will help with determining how we should respond to this needy and demanding person and maintain good stewardship with the time and resources entrusted to us.

1. *Set firm boundaries and stick to them in spite of the pressure to loosen them.* Set time limits on the frequency and duration of phone calls and office visits. Refer these people to professional counselors as soon as you realize the type of person with whom you are dealing.

2. *Deal firmly with any disruption of Bible study classes and small groups.* Establish guidelines for appropriate group behavior and hold them accountable for adhering to those guidelines. Often

these people will leave a group in which their behavior has become a problem, because in their view the group was "uncaring."

3. *Realistically assess the extent to which resources are going to be committed to the person.* Their demands will be constant and needs unending if you allow them to be.

4. *Pray for wisdom.* The Holy Spirit's leading is needed if ministry is to be effective. Pray for the person as well. We have been successful in providing prayer ministry to borderlines. However, boundaries must be set by the prayer group leader in order to maintain control. Borderlines have been known to try and dictate how the prayers were to be voiced and how the session was to be conducted. Remember that their relationship with God follows the same pattern as their relationships with others. They either feel very close to God or they are angry with Him for not doing what they expected.

5. *Borderlines have been deeply wounded by the significant people in their families of origin.* On one hand they need the experience of functioning in a healthy church family, yet on the other hand, they resist being an active part of the church family. We need to provide opportunities for them to experience health in relationships, and at the same time expect the process to be difficult, and at times most unsuccessful. Proverbs 26:12 may be

addressing this personality disorder when it says: "There is more hope for fools than for people who think they are wise."

The challenge posed by these four difficult personality types and the others listed (see chart 5-5) is an imposing one. Difficult people force us into a position of weighing the duty of care issues we owe our congregation with the demands, and often genuine, needs of the difficult person. We acknowledge that a realistic and healthy strategy needs to be in place in order to effectively meet our ministry obligations, both to the church and to the individual. The following guidelines, while not exclusive, will provide pastors and lay leaders with an operational framework in which healthy ministry can occur.

▸   Set healthy boundaries on time and availability for all helpers.

▸   Set healthy boundaries for the difficult personality defining for them appropriate behavior standards, especially as it relates to their participation in small groups.

▸   Be realistic with expectations for change. We rarely see significant change and growth in these individuals. They do have legitimate needs and, as a part of the body of Christ, they need ministry as all hurting people do. However, without firm boundaries in place, ministry to them can become counterproductive for the pastor and the church.

▸ Understand the difference between helping and rescuing. Enabling the difficult personality to persist in unhealthy patterns only reinforces their distorted view of life and what they perceive others are obligated to do for them.

▸ Be aware of hidden agendas. Difficult personalities are highly skilled at manipulation and deception. Assuming a trusting posture with them only leads to the exploitation of caring people.

▸ Recognize that difficult personalities have distorted images of God. Spiritual language and religious behavior may look like spiritual maturity, but in reality is just a camouflage for an immature relationship with God. Don't fall into the trap of believing you can persuade disordered personalities to be convinced of the truth as presented in Scripture. Remember, they are so emotionally handicapped that the integration of truth into their lives and the expected changes in behavior, attitude, and values usually do not take place. Expect to hear a lot of "Yeah, but" statements as you counsel them.

▸ Hold the difficult personality accountable for their behavior. Personal responsibility and ownership of negative, hurtful, and selfish behavior are aspects of their personalities that are missing.

▸ Model healthy behavior in relationships and hold the difficult personality accountable to do the same.

Providing a healthy example of how Christians treat one another is one of the constructive contributions the church can make in ministry to the difficult personality.

▸ Depend on the Holy Spirit to guide the ministry strategy and the healing process. Prayer for wisdom and discernment is invaluable in determining how to minister to these personalities.

Personality disordered individuals have suffered much emotional and spiritual damage in their relationships with others. It is in a healthy relational context like the Christian community that the Holy Spirit can bring the hope and healing so desperately needed in the lives of these wounded people. The extent to which we depend on the Holy Spirit's guidance and employ a strategy based on the knowledge available to us will insure a balanced ministry to them and protect our ability to minister to others.

Chart 5-1
Histrionic Personality Disorder Criteria

A pervasive pattern of excessive emotionality and attention seeking, beginning by early adulthood and present in a variety of contexts, is indicated by five or more of the following:

1. Is uncomfortable in situations in which he or she is not the center of attention

2. Interaction with others is often characterized by inappropriate, sexually seductive, or provocative behavior

3. Displays rapidly shifting and shallow expressions of emotions

4. Consistently uses physical appearance to draw attention to self

5. Has a style of speech that is excessively impressionistic and lacking in detail

6. Shows self-dramatization, theatricality, and exaggerated expression of emotion

7. Is suggestible (i.e. easily influenced by others or circumstances)

8. Considers relationships to be more intimate than they actually are

Chart 5-2
Dependent Personality Disorder Criteria

People with this disorder display a pervasive and excessive need to be taken care of that leads to submissive and clinging behavior and fears of separation, beginning by early adulthood and present in a variety of contexts, as indicated by five or more of the following:

1. Has difficulty making everyday decisions without an excessive amount of advice and reassurance from others

2. Needs others to assume responsibility for most major areas of his or her life

3. Has difficulty expressing disagreement with others because of fear of loss of support or approval
   Note: This does not include realistic fears of retribution.

4. Has difficulty initiating projects or doing things on his or her own because of a lack of self-confidence in judgment or ability rather than a lack of motivation or energy.

5. Goes to excessive lengths to obtain nurturance and support from others, to the point of volunteering to do things that are unpleasant

6. Feels uncomfortable or helpless when alone because of exaggerated fears of being unable to care for himself or herself

7. Urgently seeks another relationship as a source of care and support when a close relationship ends

8. Is unrealistically preoccupied with fears of being left to take care of himself or herself

Chart 5-3
Antisocial Personality Disorder Criteria

Characterized by a habitual disregard for social norms and rules, people suffering from this disorder lack guilty feelings when norms and rules are broken. They display exploitive, dishonest behavior, beginning by early adulthood and present in a variety of contexts, as indicated by five or more of the following.

1. Failure to conform to social norms with respect to lawful behaviors and indicated by repeatedly performing acts that are grounds for arrest

2. Deceitfulness, as indicated by repeated lying, use of aliases, or conning others for personal profit or pleasure

3. Impulsivity or failure to plan ahead

4. Irritability and aggressiveness, as indicated by repeated physical fights or assaults

5. Reckless disregard for safety of self or others

6. Consistent irresponsibility, as indicated by repeated failure to sustain consistent work behavior or honor financial obligations

7. Lack of remorse, as indicated by being indifferent to or rationalizing having hurt, mistreated, or stolen from another

Chart 5-4
Borderline Personality Disorder Criteria

This disorder includes rapid mood swings, tempestuous, interpersonal relationships with mixed feelings of love and hate, anger and elation, depression and guilt, beginning by early adulthood and present in variety of contexts, as indicated by seven or more of the following.

1. Frantic efforts to avoid real or imagined abandonment

2. A pattern of unstable and intense interpersonal relationships characterized by alternating between extremes of over idealization and devaluation

3. Identity disturbance; markedly and persistently unstable self-image or sense of self.

4. Impulsivity in at least two areas that are potentially self-damaging (e.g. spending, sex, substance abuse, reckless driving, binge eating)

5. Recurrent suicidal behavior, gestures or threats, or self-mutilating behavior

6. Affective instability due to a marked reactivity of mood (e.g. intense episodic dysphoria, irritability, or anxiety usually lasting a few hours and only rarely more than a few days)

7. Chronic feelings of emptiness or boredom

8. Inappropriate, intense anger or difficulty controlling anger (e.g. frequent displays of temper, constant anger, recurrent physical fights)

9. Transient, stress-related ideation or severe dissociative symptoms

Chart 5-5
Brief Descriptions of Other Selected Personality Disorders

Narcissistic Personality Disorder	Individuals with this disorder often have a grandiose sense of self-importance. They are known to exaggerate achievements and talents and to expect that others will recognize their special abilities. They often are preoccupied with fantasies of unlimited success, power, brilliance, beauty, or ideal love. They have a strong sense of entitlement, expecting that others will give them favorable treatment because of their status. They require constant attention and admiration. They lack empathy for the feelings of others and tend to envy those who are successful and admired.
Schizoid Personality Disorder	These individuals do not enjoy or desire close relationships, including being a part of a family. They almost always choose solitary activities and rarely experience strong emotions. They often manifest indifference to either praise or criticism from others. They are aloof and cold, rarely reciprocating gestures and facial expressions, such as smiles and nods. They have no close friends or confidants.
Avoidant Personality Disorder	Individuals with this disorder are easily hurt by criticism or disapproval. They have no close friends and are unwilling to get involved with people unless they can be certain they will be liked and accepted. They will choose to avoid social or occupational activities that involve significant interpersonal contact. They will often exaggerate the potential for difficulties, physical danger, or risks involved in doing something ordinary but not a part of their usual routine. They are fearful of being embarrassed in front of other people.

(continued on next page)

Chart 5-5
Brief Descriptions of Other Selected Personality Disorders

Obsessive-Compulsive Personality Disorder	Individuals with this disorder are often preoccupied with details, rules, lists, order, organization, or schedules to the extent that the major point of the activity is lost. They tend to be highly perfectionistic and have trouble completing tasks because of their own unrealistic expectations for meeting high standards. They are excessive in their devotion to work to the exclusion of friendships and leisure. They restrict expressions of affection and are inflexible in matters of morality, ethics, and values. They often lack generosity in giving time, money, or gifts when no personal gain is likely to result.
Paranoid Personality Disorder	An individual with this disorder will expect to be exploited or harmed by others. They tend to question the trustworthiness of friends and read hidden, demeaning, or threatening meanings into benign remarks by others. They bear grudges and are usually unforgiving of insults or slights. They often are easily slighted and quick to react with anger. They question, without justification, the fidelity and loyalty of those close to them.
Schizotypal Personality Disorder	These individuals exhibit excessive social anxiety, odd or eccentric behavior, and have few friends. Their physical appearance is usually odd and their speech is often vague or inappropriately abstract. They have unusual perceptual experiences, often sensing the presence of a force or a person not actually present. Their beliefs often include clairvoyance, telepathy, or having a "sixth sense." They exhibit inappropriate gestures or facial expressions, such as smiles and nods that do not match the situation. They are often suspicious and paranoid in their thinking.

CHAPTER 6

HELPING TROUBLED MARRIAGES

wo couples came to their pastor for marital counseling. In each case, the presenting problem was conflict over how to manage their finances. One of the couples responded to the pastor's recommendation that they seek help from a financial counselor and attend the Crown Ministry seminar offered by the church. This couple was able to work out a plan of action, implement it, and experience a reduction in the level of conflict and frustration generated by this issue in their marriage. The other couple received the same counsel, met with a financial counselor, and participated in the same seminar. Their experience was quite different from that of the other couple. They did not resolve the conflict. In fact, after the seminar they were fighting more because they had more information to fuel their conflict to even higher levels.

One of the most common requests pastors receive is for marriage counseling. There are stressors on marriage and family life that seem to remain constant from generation to generation. Each generation of pastors is called upon to help couples cope with these stressors. These include: financial pressure, health issues, sexual expectations, parenting challenges, career conflicts and demands, in-law and extended family expectations, and the constant tension between time availability and the need to nurture and care for the marital relationship. Other stressors that often come as a surprise to couples are: differences in values, behaviors, attitude, expectations, and perspective, based on personality and past life experiences. In this chapter we will identify two classifications of couples that respond quite differently to these stressors. The need to develop different strategies of ministry for "functional" and "dysfunctional" marriages is the focus of this chapter. As demonstrated by the example of the two couples in conflict over finances at the beginning of this chapter, what works for one couple may not work for another.

Pastors and the couples they serve have at their disposal a plethora of resources to help marriages and families build and maintain healthy relationships. At no time in the history of the church have there been as many resources as exist today. The number and diversity of books, videos, tapes, seminars, retreats, radio, television programs, and sermon topics is a bit overwhelming when it comes to making choices as to which will be used to help struggling couples. Couples living in urban areas usually have many Christian counselors available to them. Many churches require pre-marital preparation programs for engaged couples (which is a foundational component for strengthening marriage), and some have developed couple mentoring as a way to address helping hurting marriages. It would seem to the objective observer that with this wealth of resources that marriage and family life in this generation should be healthier than previous generations.

The evidence, however, indicates otherwise. According to a Barna study, 27 percent of born-again Christians are or have previously been divorced, compared to 24 percent of adults who are not born again.[1] Perhaps this data partly reflects the fact that many people come to the church post-divorce for help and support which is of course what we want to see happen as we operate as a "spiritual hospital" to care for the wounded. Yet it is widely accepted among those who study the issue that there seems to be no measurable difference between our society and the church when it comes to divorce rates. Many people are perplexed and confused by the large number of failed marriages we observe within the church. While the church is not responsible for the high divorce rate among Christians, we are responsible to address the problem as effectively as possible. Mike McManus goes even farther when he points out that since 75 percent of couples are married in a church, the church should therefore accept a certain amount of responsibility for the divorce rate among Christians.[2] We can all agree we have a "duty of care" to the couples in our churches to provide effective strategies for helping them deal with times of crisis in their marriages and hopefully help to reduce the divorce rate among Christians.

It has been our experience that relying on providing good enrichment programs and sound biblical teaching on the subject of marriage is not enough to move couples in crisis to a place of health and stability. Reliance on a cognitive-behavioral process proved ineffective in the case of many troubled marriages. Many churches operate from the assumption that if a couple understands what the biblical expectations for roles and behavior are, and then they will develop a healthy relationship. We therefore have worked hard to define the roles of husbands and wives, teach good communication principles, and interpret what Paul writes about in Ephesians when he says a man must love his wife as Christ loved the church and gave Himself up for it (Eph. 5:25) and a wife must respect her husband. (See Ephesians 5:33.)

We have also provided small group experiences for couples to build healthy and supportive relationships with other couples, and to facilitate accountability and opportunity for service to others. In our church, the Adult Bible Fellowship meeting on Sunday morning has been the primary resource available to couples needing to build healthy relationships with others. Small groups have developed out of the Sunday morning experience, which focus on deeper Bible study, prayer, and fellowship. These too have been beneficial for many couples seeking to strengthen their connection to other believers. The troubled marriage, however, does not seem to be able to benefit from these experiences. It seems to have trouble integrating the examples about what a healthy marriage looks like into the daily life of their own marriage.

Knowledge in and of itself does not result in a change of behavior, attitudes, and values, nor does it provide the healing and restoration that we assume its acquisition will produce. Many couples have prospered and experienced enriched relationships from the teaching and support received in their churches. However, as we noted earlier, there are really two basic classifications of marriages in our churches. One is the functional marriage and the other is the dysfunctional marriage. The functional marriage needs and benefits from enrichment programs and activities, but the dysfunctional marriage does not. It is the dysfunctional marriage that poses the greatest challenge for us in ministry. It is from among the dysfunctional marriages where the likelihood of a divorce is high. An examination of these two classifications of marriages will help us to distinguish which strategies of care and response will be most effective for each.

Symptoms that frequently drive the functional couple to seek help include: poor communication and decision making, poor conflict resolution skills, differences in parenting styles, dual career tension, sexual dissatisfaction, in-law relationships, financial stress, coping with health issues, and child behavior. The causes of these symptoms are most frequently discovered to be: poor conflict resolution skills, lack of knowledge, misplaced priorities, ineffective stress management, ineffective communication patterns, and a lack of time together.

The functional couple has a level of commitment to each other that is characteristically strong and provides a foundation upon which problem-solving strategies can be effectively implemented. These couples benefit from the resources offered to them by their church, and from couples counseling as well. Many of these couples prosper with self-paced studies using books, videos, and audiotapes. These couples are usually well motivated by the discomfort present in their relationship and are proactive in seeking help.

The dysfunctional marriage, however, is much different. The troubled couple does not seem to respond well to the help that is provided by the programs and resources of their church. If they do seek counseling, it too often seems to be ineffective in bringing about the level of healing and restoration needed. These couples can be identified by the following factors: high levels of conflict, frequent separations and threats of divorce, lack of emotional intimacy, a history of unresolved conflicts, sexual frustration, financial mismanagement, a lack of trust and respect, a history of emotional or physical abuse, expressed dissatisfaction and discouragement with their relationship in general, and often extramarital affairs. These couples are at a very high risk for divorce and require a different set of strategies to address their needs.

The educational-knowledge (cognitive-rational) based approaches that are effective with the functional couple do not seem to be generally effective for the troubled marriage. An effective strategy requires dealing with core issues of woundedness commonly inherent in the lives of one or both of the individuals in troubled marriages. Individual healing *must* occur before marital healing can be experienced. The causes of individual woundedness, often ignored by those trying to help, can be grouped under the broad categories of abuse, abandonment, and neglect. Most often these were experienced in the individual's family of origin. We also find traumatic life events experienced in adulthood, like a rape or the death of a child, inflict emotional wounds that become causal factors in marital discord. Wounded people react out of their pain to current events that are disturbing to them.

For example, we know that women who have been sexually abused as children often have difficulty controlling their anger. Any perceived threat, like a husband expressing his frustration over some aspect of her behavior, may cause him to be seen as "the enemy" and will result in more anger and conflict. It is important to identify these emotional "triggers" in order to begin to manage the anger emanating from childhood abuse. These triggers can include certain phrases, tones, volume, and inflection in voice, physical posture, physical touch, sexually-oriented comments, or something as simple as trying to awaken someone by touching them. Once these triggers are identified, both husband and wife can develop a sensitivity to them and avoid the psychological mine field they present.

Most marriage counseling in a church setting would focus on trying to improve conflict management skills and miss the fact that the conflict is a symptom of unresolved hurt in the life of one spouse. In the case of a wife who is the victim of sexual abuse in her past, the discord in the marriage related to her unresolved pain cannot be addressed in marital counseling until she experiences a level of healing both emotionally and spiritually. As we saw in chapter 4, there is often spiritual bondage present along with the emotional pain that must be recognized and addressed in the helping process. The devil exploits any woundedness and complicates the treatment plan if his influence is not eliminated.

Hurting people often choose to medicate their pain with alcohol, drugs, sex, food, work, or other compulsive behaviors (see chapter 7), which multiplies the level of stress on their marriage relationship. We discussed personality disorders in chapter 5, and these certainly can be factors in marital disharmony and dissolution. Since we recognize that it is possible for a Christian to experience demonic oppression, that too must be considered in the diagnostic process of identifying core issues and developing strategies of treatment. The focus of strategies designed to help the troubled marriage must, we believe, begin with the individual and his or her need for healing. Our assumption is that two "relatively" healthy and healed individuals can function in and contribute to a healthy and functional marital relationship.

We have learned that an effective treatment plan may include counseling, prayer team ministry, support groups, recovery groups, mentoring couples, and small group accountability. The healing model, as noted in chapter 2, is fluid and involves a dynamic interplay between the components rather than being a linear model. Healing is too complex and interdependent on too many elements to be ordered in a certain way. The spiritual component alone is a dynamic, individualized process of interaction between the Holy Spirit and the soul and spirit of the individual. In the Casas model, the pastoral counselor functions as spiritual director, case manager, coach, and as therapist, superintending and coordinating the interaction and timing of the various components.

Consider the case of John and Sue. They have been married for five years and have no children. They both have demanding careers that require fifty or more hours a week on the job. They each have been married once before. Their marriage has been characterized by constant conflict. They have been separated six times in their five years together. They have sought the help of two different marriage counselors and one pastor. They have attended a marriage conference, which was counterproductive for them and resulted in a heated argument on the way home from the conference. They are active church members and serve together in a ministry. They have outgoing personalities and relate well to those with whom they serve.

Sue was raised as an only child in a home devoid of physical nurture and love. She describes her parents as detached, cold, and consumed with their own careers. John was raised in a Christian home by parents who were regular in church attendance. His father was an alcoholic who led a double life, serving as a deacon in his church while drinking daily and verbally abusing his children and wife. John describes his home as "looking good on the outside, but messed up on the inside." Sue reports that John is moody, withdrawn, verbally abusive, angry, and blaming. He frequently uses pot to calm down and "mellow out." He has been unfaithful to her at least once during one of their separations. John describes Sue as highly controlling in all aspects of their relationship. She frequently quotes him Scripture and preaches at him with condemnation for his "sinful behavior."

John states that he feels like the enemy and is treated like he is Sue's child instead of her husband. Each describes the other as highly defensive and overreactive.

It was apparent to the counselor after the first session that this couple could not participate in a healthy way in couples counseling. Neither was able to look objectively at the situation and assume responsibility for his or her own actions. Each blamed the other for the pain and conflict in their relationship. Both agreed that counseling had not worked for them and they were very disappointed in their partner's response to the marriage conference they had attended.

John and Sue are a prime example of the dysfunction couple category. Their relationship is marked by conflict, pain, and dissatisfaction. Correctly diagnosing this couple as dysfunctional helps us develop an effective treatment plan that moves them individually toward healing and wholeness. They have tried the insight-oriented approach both in counseling and in an educational setting. Yet this approach that works so well with a functional couple is ineffective and actually counterproductive for this couple. The Casas counselor in meeting with this couple explained why their well-intentioned and commendable efforts at working on their relationship failed. The counselor explained that a focusing on the symptoms missed the core individual issues of woundedness that are the probable cause of their marital conflict and disappointment.

The counselor then recommended a counseling plan that would lead to individual healing. They were encouraged to avoid any controversial issues and show respect for one another by giving emotional space to allow for the individual work to continue without the emotional interruption produced by the constant conflict.

The setting of strict boundaries is essential for conflicted couples to be able to take the focus off of their partner's behavior and work on their own healing. Boundaries provide for a "place of safety" that helps to break the cycle of attack defend, attack defend, that is so destructive to a relationship.

As we have previously discussed, the healing model we use involves the interactive flow of counseling and prayer therapy. As soon as John and Sue were ready, they were encouraged to participate in the seven-step process to help them deal with their individual, emotional, and spiritual bondage. It has been our experience that this model is effective in getting below the surface and confronting the emotional and spiritual strongholds that exist. For example, in this case, Sue's need to control everyone and everything in her life is directly connected to her childhood of neglect. In her case, dealing with forgiving her parents and her strong self-reliance (to insure she would not be hurt again) were essential if she was to experience the individual healing that was a prerequisite to healing her marriage. The seven-step process addresses both of these issues and gives us a practical tool with which to dig below the surface and expose the wound and experience the healing ministry of the Holy Spirit.

This identification process was followed by more counseling and prayer for inner healing. The counselor and those serving on the prayer teams helped to provide, perhaps for the first time in the lives of these two wounded people, a safe, healthy, relational environment in which the damage done in an unsafe relational environment could be addressed. The entire process of healing a dysfunctional marriage is lengthy and complex. It requires a deliberate commitment on the part of the individuals to work hard and persevere in confronting the pain of the past and in the self-examination inherent in this process. It requires the church's commitment of time and human resources and perhaps even financial assistance to help cover the costs of the counseling.

If we are to be effective in helping to reduce the tragic number of divorces experienced by Christian people, then the church and its leadership must be willing to provide the resources and the means for couples to access them. If we understand that a "one size fits all" approach to helping the marriages in our churches is shortsighted and simplistic and that couples like John and Sue need a more intensive and strategically focused approach, then we will begin to address the issue of high divorce rates among Christians with more success.

The pastor who does not have professional counselors on his staff faces a challenge in developing a strategy for helping a dysfunctional couple like John and Sue. It is essential in that situation for the pastor to identify Christian counselors with whom he can work to develop a comprehensive strategy incorporating the prayer ministry of the church with the professional counseling process. Many churches have counselors in their membership who could and would eagerly participate in a coordinated plan to help those hurting in troubled marriages experience healing individually and relationally. A dialogue between pastors and Christian counselors regarding strategy development is a place to start to insure the issue of divorce in the church is given the attention it demands.

The troubling divorce rate among Christians is a wake-up call to both the church and Christian counselors that new strategies need to be devised and implemented, and more collaboration between the two put in place if we are to see a decline in the number of divorces experienced in the Christian community.

Chart 6-1 Marriages: Functional and Dysfunctional	
Functional	**Presenting symptoms:** poor communication and decision making, elevated conflict, differences in parenting style, dual career tension, sexual dissatisfaction, conflict over in-law relationships, financial stress caused by poor money management, health issues, child behavior
	Probable causes: poor communication skills, ineffective conflict resolution skills, lack of knowledge, need for training (i.e., parenting), ineffective stress management, lack of time together, differing values and beliefs, unmet expectations
Dysfunctional	**Presenting symptoms:** high levels of conflict, frequent separations, threats of divorce, lack of emotional intimacy, history of unresolved conflicts, sexual frustration, lack of trust and respect, history of emotional or physical abuse, poor money management, extramarital affairs
	Probable causes: childhood trauma including abuse, abandonment, neglect; adult trauma including rape, death of a child, accident or injury, abusive relationships

CHAPTER 7

HELPING THE ADDICTED

The addicted person presents a significant challenge for most pastors and churches in two primary ways. First, there is confusion on how to separate the sin from the sinner. Addiction to alcohol, drugs, pornography, gambling, food, and work are frequently encountered in the counseling experience of the pastor. Approximately fourteen million Americans—7.4 percent of the population—meet the diagnostic criteria for alcohol abuse or alcoholism. More than one-half of American adults have a close family member who either has or has had alcoholism. It is also reported that approximately one in four children younger than eighteen-years-old in the United States is exposed to alcohol abuse or alcohol dependence in his family.[1]

In 2000, an estimated 1.2 million Americans were current cocaine users. Approximately 2.5 million Americans use marijuana for the first time each year. It is the most commonly used illicit drug. As reported in 2000, 76 percent of illicit drug users consumed only marijuana.[2]

Historically, the church has been ineffective in providing ministry to addicts. In part this is due to strong negative reactions toward the behaviors emanating from the addiction. The pain inflicted upon families and friends by the addict's behavior contributes to a negative bias against the offender, and calls attention to the pain existent in the family system. The addict's family often asks for help before the addict is ready to do so. The pastor who hears the story of how much pain and damage has been inflicted on family members is set up in a sense to negatively view the perpetrator of the wounds inflicted. The message received by most addicts is that they are not welcome in the church and therefore they are understandably reluctant to seek help from the church. Addicts are a marginalized segment of society. The response of many churches to the addict merely reflects what is seen in society.

The second reason for the church's difficulty with helping addicts is confusion on regarding how to best help those caught up in the web of addiction. The resources needed to deal with addicts far exceed most church's ability to provide. Treatment is costly and complex, requiring the expertise of professionals in many disciplines. Most pastors refer addicts to treatment or rehabilitation centers and pray that the process will be successful. Some churches have identified a way in which they can be directly involved in helping addicts that is within their scope of spiritual ministry. Recovery programs provide a means for churches to build a bridge between the addict and the ministries of the church. Church-based recovery programs are an effective means of helping communities address a serious social issue. They can become a point of connectedness between churches and community resources united by a desire to help addicts and their families move into successful recovery.

Recovery has a biblical parallel in the concept of sanctification. Common ground between these two can be identified by the components of honest introspection, acceptance of a fallen condition, recognition of a need for forgiveness, acknowledgment of a need for saving grace, and a realization that the process cannot be completed based on one's own strength. Both involve bringing grace into a life dominated by denial, guilt, shame, and self-protection. Recovery and sanctification both seek to move a person from a place of hiding from God to a place of knowing Him and accepting His unconditional love. In this author's opinion, the church is perhaps the most powerful resource available to addicts. It can provide the spiritual and human resources needed for a healthy recovery.

Addicts will respond to churches that are accepting and live out grace by offering unconditional love. Addicts need acceptance to counter the intense feelings of shame and guilt they feel toward themselves. Perhaps the most effective way to communicate acceptance is by providing effective support groups. At Casas, we have selected the Celebrate Recovery model, developed by Saddleback Community Church. Offering effective help to addicts is becoming more common as thousands of churches have started recovery programs within the last ten years.[3] Fuller Theological Seminary has established The Institute of Recovery Ministry and is offering degrees in Recovery Ministry.[4] Some churches are characterized as "recovery churches" and have established ministries that reach addicts with the truth that there is hope in their relationship with God. Dale Ryan quotes a seminary professor who told him, "Having a recovery ministry had rapidly become a basic essential for any evangelical church."[5]

Addicts often see themselves as modern-day lepers—outcasts who people would rather avoid than confront. We know from the earthly ministry of Jesus to lepers and other outcasts that if He were on Earth today, He would be meeting addicts at the point of their need with unconditional love. The church can continue Jesus' ministry to the disenfranchised—the addict—and express His unconditional love by providing for healthy recovery following treatment. The extent to which we as the church can partner with treatment centers and become a strategic component of healthy follow-up care will enhance the likelihood of successful recovery for many addicts.

Addicts will also respond to churches that are emotionally safe for them. Churches that offer recovery ministries will be perceived as safe, or at least the recovery program will be perceived as safe, and will be a doorway into the life of the church. A safe church is one that exhibits a patient, grace-filled attitude toward people's mistakes. A safe church is giving and gentle, cares more about authenticity (being open about one's own failures, shortcomings, and weaknesses, instead of conveying an attitude of "we have it all together and you don't") than protecting an image. A safe church values honesty and seeks to resolve conflicts in healthy ways. Casas is working in an intentional way to be a healthy church for every one of its people. (See Appendix G for the Casas Statement on Health.)

Addicts need a church that is balanced in its focus, ministry, doctrine, and relationships. A balanced, healthy church is important because the addict's life has been so out of balance. A balanced, healthy church provides the addict with a safe place to work on his or her most difficult spiritual issue—developing a trust in God. Historically, addicts have little or no trust in God or in those who represent God. When addicts experience acceptance from a pastor who models a servant leadership rather than an authoritative style, the door is open for them to then address their relationship with God. Experiencing graceful shepherding is like salve on a wound to most addicts and is a perquisite to learning how to trust God. The pastor is the key to establishing an accepting climate within the church. Addicts will respond to a pastor who identifies himself and his church as being in need of God's grace and forgiveness. He must clearly communicate that the ground is always level at the foot of the cross.

A relapse into a loss of sobriety could, in some settings, bring condemnation and judgment on the addict. If the spiritual and emotional climate in a church is accepting and recognizes we all fall short at times, then the addict can accept his or her failure to maintain sobriety as a consequence of innate human weakness, a condition shared by all of us. As with any other sin, there are consequences to addiction that must also be faced honestly and realistically. Helping an addict deal with those consequences is precisely where the church can demonstrate a forgiving attitude, establish a climate of safety, and hold the addict accountable for wrong behavior. Addicts need churches that will hold them accountable for their behavior in the context of a relationship with another person. Churches that have strong discipleship programs, as well as recovery programs, offer structure within relational contexts in which accountability for spiritual growth can take place. Addicts need both biblical teaching and modeling on what righteous living looks like as it is expressed in an individual life. There is no substitute for personal accountability, however, an individual or group can help to hold the course of a healthy recovery. Accountability addresses the need for acceptance and belonging, which is so often absent in the addict's family of origin. The process teaches the addict how to establish and maintain healthy boundaries in relationships with others. Churches with recovery programs soon learn that accountability is something we all—not just addicts—need as we grow in our Christian experience.

The church can also assume a primary role in the recovery process by providing the follow-up care component, which follows the treatment that preferably takes place in a formal rehabilitation or treatment setting. If, as is often the case, the cost of inpatient treatment is prohibitive, the individual has the option of outpatient programs or Alcoholics Anonymous, Narcotics Anonymous, Gamblers Anonymous, Sex Anonymous, Overeaters Anonymous, and any twelve-step group focused on a specific addiction. Formal treatment should be encouraged as it deals with issues—like the reasons for medicating pain—that are critical to the recovery process. One of the issues not addressed in secular treatment programs is spiritual bondage. The church is equipped to deal with this important core issue and can make a significant contribution to successful recovery in doing so.

A comprehensive follow-up care plan provided by the church should include a recovery program like Celebrate Recovery with structure, operational guidelines, and an established curriculum. Individual, marriage, and family counseling, if not available from a church-based counseling ministry, could be provided by a subsidy arrangement with the Christian counseling community. Prayer teams organized and trained to deal with the spiritual bondage issues associated with addiction are crucial to the long-term viability of successful follow-up care and the recovery process. As we previously discussed in chapter 4, the seven-step model is an effective tool to address spiritual bondage and is compatible with the twelve-step recovery process. The dramatic difference in success rates between secular and Christian treatment programs emphasizes the crucial importance of the spiritual component. Teen Challenge reports approximately 85 percent of their graduates maintain successful recovery while most secular programs report 15 to 20 percent success rates.[6]

It is reasonable to assume that addictions will continue to be a major social and medical issue. The church must assume its responsibility as a place of healing and wholeness for those struggling with addictions and their families. A discussion of addictions cannot be complete without pointing out that sexual addiction is gaining momentum. Addiction experts, like Patrick Carnes, predict that this will soon surpass alcoholism as the addiction of choice in Americans.[7] The dramatic rise in sexual addiction has been fueled by the easy access to sexually explicit material on the Internet. Sex-related terms are the number one search topic on the Internet, with more than twenty million people visiting sexually oriented Internet sites per month.[8]

Christians are not immune to the lure and temptation of Internet pornography. The church must be aware of the seriousness and pervasiveness of pornography and other forms of sexual addiction in order to educate and warn, as well as help, those caught in the trap to get free. Sexual addiction, like all addictions, is based on a need to medicate pain. Loneliness, rejection, abuse, neglect, and abandonment are the primary motivators of pain relief. The comfort sought and found in the unhealthy expression of one's sexuality reinforces the cycle of pain and relief prevalent in the life of the addict. Sexual addiction has the same chemical component as all addictions. The brain gets addicted to the chemical high produced by sexual behavior, and recovery is therefore complicated by the need to establish new neuropathways. This process is enhanced by breaking the cycle of pain relief with new, healthy behaviors.

The church can be effective in helping the addict adopt and practice healthy behaviors and thought patterns. The spiritual bondage produced by the habitual practice of seeking relief and pleasure in the sexual arena must be broken if freedom is to be experienced. At the core of the spiritual bondage of sexual addiction is idolatry in its raw form. Our culture, like that of the Corinthians and Ephesians of Paul's day, practices idolatry using sexuality as its focus. The idol comforts them, celebrates with them, and is available at all times to meet their need for comfort and pleasurable relief from pain. The impact of this addiction on the individual, their marriages, and families is devastating. Pastors are encouraged to inform and educate themselves as to the epidemic proportions of this addiction and its impact on the church.

A visit to the Web site of Christian Recovery International (www.christianrecovery.com) will provide links to a number of helpful resources. Dr. Patrick Carnes is recognized as one of the pioneers in the study of sexual addiction. A study of his work is recommended as a foundational and reliable means of understanding this subject.[9] Pastors also need to be aware of their own vulnerability. A survey of evangelical Protestant clergy in the United States found that 40 percent of the respondents admitted that they struggled with pornography, largely obtained through the Internet.[10] John Baker, pastor of recovery at Saddleback Community Church, has, in conjunction with the promotion of Celebrate Recovery, discovered that many pastors need help with their own struggle with pornography. He offers help in connecting hurting pastors to therapeutic resources via his e-mail: johnb@saddleback.net. Dr. Mark Laaser has written extensively on the subject of sexual addiction within clergy and reports that the number of clergy of all religious traditions struggling with Internet pornography is increasing.[11]

Recovery material and programs specific to sexual addiction are available to churches. Recovery groups offer a means to bring accountability and discipleship to those seeking to establish a righteous lifestyle. Educating the congregation about sexual addiction and its insidious nature is vitally important. A stern warning needs to be given to the youth of the church who are at high risk and vulnerable to the lure of the sexually explicit material. Our youth also can benefit from effective educational programs that teach what healthy sexuality looks like from a biblical perspective. A referral network needs to be established with the Christian counseling community, so as to facilitate connecting those struggling with this addiction to get the individual attention they need. Like all addictions, sexual addiction needs to be addressed by the church in a way that is sensitive to the need for grace, mercy, and forgiveness. Prayer teams can be so helpful to minister all three of these and facilitate the healing power of the Holy Spirit.

Recovery programs emphasizing sobriety, serenity, and service are appropriate ministries for churches. As the church empowered, we can offer the best of alternatives to the unhealthy ways people seek to have their needs met by their drugs of choice. We can offer healthy ways for our members to feel good about themselves, such as understanding who we are in Christ and discovering meaning and purpose in life through service to others. We have learned that nothing says "I am accepted" like being invited to join a ministry in service to others. Healing and recovery occur in the interaction of a willing, obedient, seeking person with a caring community of fellow strugglers, empowered by the grace, mercy, and forgiveness of the Lord Jesus Christ. It is no longer an option for the church to remain idle and uninvolved when we have so much to offer to so many who are in captivity to addictions.

CHAPTER 8

DEALING WITH DISTORTED IMAGES OF GOD

O ver the years in working with hurting people, we have learned that most, if not all, struggle with a distorted image of God. This distortion blocks their spiritual growth and contributes to faulty thinking about how God sees them and they see God. While many wounded people suffer from a distorted view of God, it is also true that many Christians who do not view themselves as wounded suffer from the same malady. It is therefore crucial that pastors and teachers address this subject in sermons, as it is seminal in the development of Christian maturity. We have been alerted to the need to address this issue in the lives of wounded people through the Christian Recovery movement. Juanita Ryan has written extensively on this subject, and has much to contribute to our understanding of how to facilitate healing of distortions in our view of God.[1]

From her work, we learn that hurting people will be impacted by their distorted images of God in three primary ways. First, their view of God affects and determines the direction of their spiritual growth. For example, a person who believes God is distant and emotionally detached will have little incentive to connect with God on anything other than an intellectual level. As one man to whom we ministered stated: "Why try and work on a relationship with someone who seems so disinterested?" Those who perceive God in this way often lack energy and motivation and are devoid of passion in their pursuit of God. They are the "pew sitters" who maintain a spectator orientation in their relationship to God and the work of the church. In some respects they live vicariously off of the faith of others and express confusion as to how some people can be so close to God.

Second, it therefore follows that for a person with this view, motivation regarding spiritual things and church life is hindered significantly. If a person sees God as distant and aloof, then there is little motivation to participate in a small group Bible study, a worship seminar, or attend a prayer meeting. Perhaps a distorted image of God is one of the causal factors that help explain the prayerlessness present in most North American evangelical churches. In our experience, prayer meetings are the poorest attended of all church meetings. Prayer assumes a relationship exists between the pray-er and God and that the relationship is based on faith and trust. For many who sit in our pews on Sundays, this is not the case. Many know about God and accept the theology they are taught intellectually but have not experienced Him at a level that is highly relational.

Third, a person's image of God and his relationship with Him impacts his self-image. A person who sees God as distant and emotionally absent is likely to view himself as having little value or worth. One person we worked with expressed it this way: "When God was passing out natural talents and abilities and spiritual gifts, He passed me by. I don't think He even saw me." After years of attending church, she never experienced the joy and excitement in her Christian life that comes from giving to others in Jesus' name. She did not give because her view of God led her to believe she had nothing to offer. She saw herself as a child of God; an abandoned and ignored child, not a loved and cherished one. Her view of her value and worth before God was so distorted that she was unable to accept that she had some unusual abilities in one area of her life that would have allowed her to prosper in a career. Her self-image was directly related to how she perceived God's "failure" to love her. Her life decisions were based on these distortions and resulted in a misuse of her God-given abilities.

Distortions in our view of God come from three primary sources. The most common is parenting. Parents and parental figures exert a powerful influence over the formation of a child's image of God. If a parent is emotionally or physically absent, then it is likely that the child's view of God will be that He too is absent and uninvolved. J. B. Phillips, in his classic book *Your God Is Too Small*, wrote about this correlation between parents and God. He believed that how a person was parented had a profound influence over how God was perceived.[2]

Tragic life events are, in our experience, probably the second most influential factor in the formation of one's image of God. Tragic life events, like the death of a child, a murder, a rape, an accident that resulted in paralysis, or severe childhood abuse, are often interpreted as having happened under God's control. Because He had control and didn't stop the tragedy, this line of thinking goes, "He must therefore not care or else He must be really mean and cruel to allow such events to occur." It also follows that many conclude that God does not love them because a loving heavenly father would not allow anything to hurt His children. It is not surprising that a person who doesn't feel loved and protected by God would distance himself from Him and the church that represents Him.

Early in this author's counseling experience, I met a man with such a distorted view of God. As a nineteen-year-old Marine medic kneeling in the blood-soaked sands of Iwo Jima during World War II, he concluded that if God truly were a loving heavenly Father, He would not allow the hell he was experiencing to exist on this earth. He lived his life distanced from God, medicating his pain with alcohol until his death due to alcoholism thirty-two years later. How tragic that his distorted view of God was so pervasive that it dictated how he lived his life and how he chose to handle his pain! Distortions like this are common among the people and their families that we minister to in churches. Our challenge is to lovingly and carefully address their faulty theology and negative emotions. The difficulty we face is that, while we have the answers to their questions about who God is, we don't often get the opportunity to help them because of their own rejection of the church.

A third major contributor to a distorted image of God is experiences with religion and churches. A person who has experienced spiritual abuse at the hands of a religious leader who "spoke for God" will likely have a distorted view about who God is as a result. Some examples from our experience include:

▸ A pastor who told a woman who was being physically abused by her husband that God wanted her to stay and endure the abuse because it was an act of obedience to Him and that He would change her husband.

▸ Church leadership who assumed control over the members to the extent that permission and "blessings" had to be obtained from them prior to getting married, changing jobs, or buying a house.

▸ A church that taught that God is punitive, and that for every sin committed you should receive corresponding levels of punishment. If something bad happened it was always because God was punishing the sinner.

▸ A church that taught that God's blessings, approval, love, and salvation are all conditional based upon one's performance.

The constant striving to be good enough to deserve God's love and grace usually results in either more compulsive achieving efforts or the realization that one can't ever measure up and therefore leaving "religion" altogether. A friend who works with female addicts observed that those who had no background in religion are much less angry at God than those who have come out of false or distorted church teachings. When we ask people who have had experiences with one of these three primary causes of a distorted image of God to describe their own view of God, their answers tend to fall into one of four categories.

1. *They see God as a policeman*—an enforcer who will exact punishment for any wrongdoing. God's job is

to always be on the lookout for those who violate His laws, to catch them, and see that they are punished. Statements like: "I know that God is angry with me and is going to punish me for what I did," "If I don't follow God's laws, I will be in trouble with Him," and, "The thing I fear worst is the wrath of God," are indicative of the policeman image of God.

2. *They see God as disapproving, rejecting, critical, and perfectionistic.* People with this view describe God with statements like: "I can never do it well enough to please Him, so why try?" "He is never satisfied with me and is always disappointed with how I do things," or, "I don't trust Him and I don't like Him."

3. *They see God as absent or distant.* This distortion can be detected by statements like: "God does not know that I exist," "Yes, God exists, but He is not really involved in my life," and, "He just sets things in motion and lets them run by themselves."

4. *They see God as a tyrant.* As one person put it, "He acts without reason to make my life miserable." Another stated, "God must really hate us, just look at all of the horrible things that happen to people."

There are also other indicators that a person is dealing with distortions in how they view God. Asking a lot of "why" questions reveals confusion, disappointment, and anger. The question, "Why didn't God stop him from drinking too much? Then the accident would not have happened?" is unanswerable. "Why" questions are like running on a treadmill; lots of energy is expended, but the runner doesn't get anywhere. "Where" questions are also difficult, if not impossible, to answer, but yet are to be expected as people struggle to understand God's role in their lives.

A rape victim once asked me during a counseling session, "Where was Jesus when I was being raped?" The answer did not come from some predetermined theological understanding or counseling training but rather from the Holy Spirit who wanted this young woman to understand God had not abandoned her in her time of crisis. The answer was: "Jesus was weeping for you!" It was the exact answer that she needed to hear in order to allow her to continue to grow in her relationship with God.

I keep a photograph in my office of the "Weeping Jesus" statue at the Oklahoma City bombing site. It serves as a visual reminder of the compassion Jesus has for the suffering of those He loves today, just as He did for Mary and Martha when their brother died as recorded in John 11:33–36. While in most cases it has been our experience that "why" and "where" questions are difficult to answer and attempts to do so are usually not productive (with a few exceptions, such as in the case just noted), it is possible for us to answer "what" questions. These are very helpful in our attempt to deal with distorted images of God. Questions like: "What does God want me to do with all this pain?" "What do I need to do to heal?" and, "What is a healthy image of God?" can all be answered in the context of a healing relationship. It has been our experience that "what" questions are most effectively answered when the focus is placed on Jesus as we understand Him from the descriptions of His earthly ministry as found in the Gospels.

Fear is another indicator of a distorted image of God. A fear of being hurt and rejected often leads someone to place safety, both emotional and spiritual, above faith. When being safe dominates one's relationship with God as well as others, it places a limit on the extent to which those relationships can grow and mature. Such a focus places false and unrealistic expectations on God and others who are trying to help. It sets God and others up for failure, in that the individual often distorts the events of life to correspond to the rejection he perceives. He may even sabotage his own progress so he can say, "See, I told you so."

A lack of trust is often coupled with fear, which contributes to a person being "frozen" in his relationships with God and others. One person, who had been rejected by every significant person in her life, put it this way: "How can I trust God, or anyone else for that matter, when I have never experienced acceptance and unconditional love in a close relationship?" The trust issue in her life manifested itself as she maintained distance between herself and others. She resisted being connected to the community of believers in any small group format and chose instead to attend only the preaching portion of Sunday services. It was interesting to note that in her case (as well as others I have observed) the worship through music part of the service was too uncomfortable for her to take part in. Perhaps this avoidance speaks to the intensely relational component of worship and to her lack of trust in her relationship with God.

A lack of joy and gratitude can be an indication that there is a distortion in the way someone perceives God. Many hurting people struggle to manage the pain of the past to such an extent that they miss positive aspects of their present lives. The pain seems to blind the wounded person to the reality that God is a part of their lives and is actively working to bring good out of the suffering they have and are experiencing. They do not see God as their strength and helper in times of trouble; rather they perceive Him as uninterested, distant, and aloof to their plight.

It doesn't take a new minister long to discover that many who attend Bible studies and teaching times don't seem to be able to integrate the truth as it is taught into their lives in an practical and observable way. The reality is that spiritual growth does not easily take place in the lives of those who have emotional woundedness. If a person filters truth as revealed in Scripture through the pain of a traumatic past, fear of rejection, or a lack of trust, the result is likely to be a distortion of that truth and a corresponding inability to apply it to his life. (See chart 8-1.) For example, a wounded person hears a sermon on unconditional love based on the story of the prodigal son. He filters the truth as it is taught through his own experiences with rejection and abandonment by his parents. The truth gets clogged in the filter by the pain that exists, and a distortion in the form of a lie is established in his mind.

The lie might take the form of unbelief: "God would never come running to greet me like the prodigal son's father did. I am not worthy of that kind of response." When we can identify the lies that shape the distortion, then we can develop a strategy for how to help the person get free of the influence of the lies. Pastors and Bible teachers often experience frustration when, after communicating truth as effectively as they know how, they see no positive results in the lives of the students. This frustration is increased by the assumption that the teaching of more truth will somehow result in a breakthrough and their students will finally "get it." It is important to realize that the causes of the students' inability to assimilate truth into their lives must be addressed in a way that results in healing and freedom.

The process of healing the causes of distortions should include the following:

Identify the distortions

Hurting people seem to respond best to dealing with their pain in the context of a helping relationship with a person they respect and can begin to trust. The pastoral counseling setting is often most effective in uncovering the painful wounds that cause the distortions. Because the damage often occurred in a relational context, healing must also take place in the setting of a safe, healthy, confidential relationship. We have learned that confidentiality is a key to effectively identifying the distortions because of the shame people feel in admitting that trusting God is something they can't seem to accomplish. It is rare that a person will deal with how he or she sees God in a small group Bible study when others in the group seem to "have it together with God."

Ask God to heal the distortions

We must recognize our dependence on the Holy Spirit for healing. The woundedness often goes so deep that our cognitive understanding will take us only so far in the healing process. We address the trust issues when we admit we are powerless to accomplish the healing necessary for a person to experience healthy relationships with God and others and ask God to help us. The Holy Spirit knows how to intercede and pray for us when we don't know how to pray for ourselves. (See Romans 8:26.)

Understand the causes of the distortions

It helps to ask questions to determine how the distortions got rooted in the person's mind. What were the experiences that inflicted the wounds that are still so painful? It is helpful to see the connections between the experiences and the distortions they produce. For example, a person who lived with a critical, emotionally distant father is helped when she begins to see how that relationship impacted her own view of God.

Build a relationship with a safe person

It is imperative that wounded people be in relationship with a safe person. A climate of emotional-relational safety is the context in which healing can best occur. As trust is established with a caring helper, the help-ee can begin to see and experience how the same process can take place with God. This process often takes a significant amount of time. It is therefore wise to refer the person to helpers—either professional or lay counselors—who can invest the time needed to insure good results.

Connecting with the church

It is just as important for the wounded person to be connected to the Christian community as it is to be connected to a caring helper. The sense of "family" that so many have lacked in their own life experience can be established by belonging to a caring and supportive group of believers, assuming those believers are relatively healthy themselves. Wounded people seem to assume everyone else has it together and are often disappointed to experience rejection from those they expected to accept and love them. The healing process is enhanced and enriched by a sense of belonging and acceptance that can take place in the Christian community. The principle we have learned is if the damage occurred in relationship with significant people, then healing must occur in relationship with caring and loving people. A functional, spiritual family is a great replacement for a dysfunctional family of origin.

Choosing the truth

It is the responsibility of the individual to choose truth as an act of willful, volitional obedience to God. If healing is to occur, the individual must accept their role in the process. The process, as we have observed it and participated in it, is a partnership between the individual and the Holy Spirit, facilitated by the ministry of the church. The process of helping and healing is something we do *with* a person not *to* a person. It is a process in which the Holy Spirit empowers, the individual obeys, and the church cares!

Commit to do the work

The individual must also commit to do the hard work of applying the truth and taking negative thoughts captive. For example, one of the homework assignments given early in the process is to read daily the Because God Loves Me handout. (See Appendix H.) The daily infusion of truth about who God is and how He sees us as His children is essential spiritual food. Learning how to pray is often difficult for people struggling with issues of trust and perceived distance from God. However there is always a starting point. We encourage the individual to start with a simple prayer such as, *God please help me today.* Using patterned prayers and writing letters to God are also helpful in developing healthy communication with God. Learning to pray Scripture, *God please give me spiritual wisdom and understanding* (Eph. 1:17) has also been powerful as the person experiences Scripture personally and experiences more comfort in praying.

The pastor or teacher, along with lay and professional helpers, and the supportive, caring ministry of the community of believers play a significant role in helping those distanced from God to develop a healthy relationship with Him. It helps the alienated person to be validated from the pulpit. This occurs when the pastor or teacher explains that we are all "in process" in our understanding of God and that no one has a perfect relationship with Him. In fact, as believers, we are all on the same path, just at different levels of growth.

The person distanced from God needs to feel like he is a part of the body. He needs to learn that he is not different and strange because he doesn't feel the same way about God or use the same language to describe his relationship with Him that others do. The pastor or teacher can help to bring a fearful, distrusting person into the sphere of the fellowship of the body by carefully addressing the issue of distorted images of God from the pulpit. Often people who are struggling with their relationship with God will connect with the church at a Sunday morning service because it is perceived as less threatening than attending a small Bible study. It is therefore important to address the issue of distorted images of God from the pulpit in a way that draws out the alienated and encourages them to connect with others who can help them in the process of healing and growth.

Chart 8-1 Truth, Filters, and Distortions	
Biblical Truth	God is loving and caring; good and merciful; giver of unconditional love; present and available; freeing; nurturing; accepting; just, fair, and impartial; steadfast and reliable; loving with discipline.
Life Experience Filters	**Childhood trauma:** abuse, abandonment, neglect by parents and caregivers
	Adult trauma: rape, death of a child, injury, illness
	Spiritual abuse: unhealthy churches, cults, false religions, the occult, New Age, Native American religions
Distortions	God is distant and aloof; mean and unloving; loves conditionally; absent when needed; a policeman—enforcer; critical and unpleasable; rejecting and perfectionistic; unjust and partial; unpredictable and untrustworthy; harsh and punitive

CHAPTER 9

DEALING WITH UNCHANGEABLE FAMILY ISSUES

Many hurting people coming to the church for help are dealing with unchangeable issues in their family, which is stressful and troublesome. For example, a spouse living with frequent rages and verbal abuse from their mate struggles with how he or she is to respond when the outbursts are directed toward them with blame and shame. Living with the possibility of being labeled the enemy and being made the scapegoat for all that is frustrating in the life of one's spouse is burdensome and defeating. The questions and statements posed to the pastor or counselor may include: "What am I to do when he rages, blames, and shames me?" "My spouse refuses to seek counsel or to accept any responsibility for her behavior," "He acts as if everything is my fault," "How am I to deal with this situation?" and, "What does the Bible say about me having to live with an emotionally abusive spouse?" In order to provide a person in a situation like this with some direction, we have identified eleven practical principles to help deal with unchangeable family situations.[1] (See Appendix I.)

Acknowledge that only God can change another person

When faced with behaviors we don't like in another, it is common to attempt to affect a change by something we do or say. In family settings this often will be expressed by lecturing, preaching, quoting Scripture, begging, threatening, giving them a book to read that addresses the issues, and setting up counseling appointments without their agreement. This process usually results in an emotional roller-coaster ride, getting one's hopes raised and then having them dashed on the "rocks of reality." People change only when they accept responsibility for their own behavior and when the pain of not changing exceeds the pain of the status quo. It often comes as a great revelation to the "fixer" that there is nothing they can do or say to change another person and that is not their responsibility to do so. When we acknowledge God as the change agent (2 Cor. 3:18) and release the other person into His care, we experience freedom from a burden He does not intend for us to carry. The focus then shifts from "fixer" to responder; from asking, "Why doesn't he change?" to, "What does a healthy response from me look like in this situation?"

Be accountable to God for how you respond to others

It is a common response for many of us to react too quickly and too sharply to the unacceptable behavior of another. The offended person's reactions are often just as unhealthy as the offender's actions. When someone can shift emotional gears by taking responsibility for his own behavior and develop a response rather than a reaction to a situation, movement toward health occurs. Responding implies that a prayerful, rational approach is being applied. Responding means one has exercised self-control and thereby allowed the Holy Spirit an opportunity to be able to work redemptively in the lives of others. (See Ephesians 4:2–3.)

Concentrate on what you can change—
your thoughts, behaviors, and attitudes

Paul admonished the Ephesians (Eph. 4:23) to take personal responsibility for their own actions toward others. This is a necessity if we are to experience a spiritual renewal of our thoughts and attitudes. When a person, in partnership with the Holy Spirit, addresses his own negative contributions to the relational climate, a positive move toward restoration can occur. Often only one party in a relationship is working on his responses and seeking the help of God to change his heart. It is important to emphasize to him that progress is being made even if it occurs only in the life of one person. Waiting for a reciprocal, positive response from another usually results in stagnation of the process of change and restoration because it takes the focus off of what one is responsible for and places it on the other person.

Pray specifically and in accordance with Scripture

As Christians, we acknowledge that an active, focused prayer life has a powerful influence on the course of our lives. Prayer is a source of great strength as we seek to cope with stressful circumstances. Effective prayer involves focusing on specific targets. For example, if one is experiencing or observing the powerful negative effects of things like confusion, hostility, rebellion, unbelief, denial, or deception in the life of a family member, it is important to specifically focus on that effect until one senses a release or change in the circumstances. Praying Scripture is a way of staying focused on one specific issue and insuring the prayer agenda is God-centered and not self-centered. If someone is observing denial in a family member, then selecting relevant scriptures pertaining to denial and using them as the structure of prayers ensures the target stays in focus, thereby increasing the effectiveness of the prayer. It is also important to take into account the work of the enemy in the life of another, and to pray spiritual warfare prayers on their behalf.[2]

Develop a strong inner life of devotion
An effective prayer life plus time spent learning from Scripture and being comforted by it provides the foundation for living victoriously both emotionally and spiritually, even in the midst of suffering and disappointment. (See Psalm 119:48.) Christians have an abundance of resources to aid them in establishing a solid devotional life. I like to start people with Henry Blackaby and Claude King's *Experiencing God* workbook, as I find this study foundational to a healthy relationship with God.[3]

Accept things as they are
When a person can move toward accepting the current situation as being outside her control, along with releasing her concerns to God, she can often experience a sense of release and a corresponding renewal of emotional energy. (See Romans 12:12–21.) It is important to understand that accepting a person or a situation does not mean liking the behavior or circumstances or understanding why they exist. Acceptance is crucial in order to cope in an effective and healthy way with difficult circumstances. Accepting the reality that this is the way it is and it may never change is healthy. It is healthy to look honestly at the issues and face the often unpleasant and discouraging reality that things are not what they should be and may never change to one's

preferences. An honest, realistic look at circumstances provides for objective clarity, which is necessary for the development of effective coping strategies.

Suffering isn't bad; it just hurts

We are all conditioned to avoid pain. It follows that we are likely to label relational pain and suffering as bad, or awful, or unfair. It is difficult for many of us to accept the reality that relationships often produce pain and suffering. When we can experience God using our suffering for our good and the good of others, then we can see purpose in it and accept its place in our lives. (See Romans 8:28.) This concept is one of the emotional and spiritual handholds one can cling to when faced with frequent hurtful behaviors in the context of close relationships. Please note that I am *not* saying a person being physically or sexually abused should just accept the reality that it is happening and do nothing about it. Appropriate action must be taken under the guidance of a pastor or counselor to insure safety from harm.

Stay connected to a Christian support system

Hurting people need God's provision in their lives, and they certainly need the caring support of others. (See Hebrews 10:25.) The church is equipped to provide the emotional and spiritual support needed by those dealing with ongoing stressful family relationships. Counselors need to encourage their clients to establish and maintain connection to Christian community. Bible studies, prayer groups, support groups, and more focused and comprehensive ministries, such as women's ministries, are essential components in insuring effective coping.

Maintain self-control

Maintaining self-control is foundational for successful coping. It is one of the issues that is clearly the responsibility of the offended person. Maintaining self-control contributes to conflict management and minimizes the level and frequency of relational conflict. Self-control flows out of a relationship with Jesus Christ as one of the fruits of the Spirit and is indicative of His influence and power in a Christian's life. (See Galatians 5:23.) The process of maintaining self-control involves behavioral control that the individual is responsible for as well as dependence on God to provide the power to sustain it and insure its continuity in one's life.

Avoid "if only" thinking

Hurting people look naturally and predictably for escape routes. One of the most common is "if only" thinking. "If only he would go to counseling with me, then things would change." "If only my child were healthy, then we could have a normal life." "If only I hadn't been laid off, then I would not be in this financial crisis." This kind of thinking is a lot like running on a treadmill; much time and energy is expended without getting anywhere. Encouraging people to take these negative and unproductive thoughts captive will reduce the stress induced by comparing how bad things are with how good they could be. (See 2 Corinthians 10:5.) A healthy response is one that avoids fantasy and addresses the reality of the circumstances with strategies that insure effective coping. "If only" thinking is obviously not a walk of faith. Releasing the circumstances and the people involved to God and trusting Him to work in the midst of suffering, confusion, and discouragement is putting faith into action. Guiding a hurting person in this way helps them to recognize and experience a disciplined walk of faith.

Be assertive and focused in applying your strategy

It is important to emphasize that without hard work, coping in a healthy way will not occur. In 1 Chronicles 22:16, we find an admonishment that fits well: "Now begin the work, and the LORD be with you" (NIV). When a strategy is developed and applied consistently, positive results are likely to be experienced. Positive reinforcement encourages and motivates a person to continue the hard work necessary to insure success. The goal for those living with stressful, unchanging family issues is to move from feeling like a victim of unjust circumstances to a place where experiencing some level of comfort with being a survivor is possible. From there, the goal is to grow to a place where victorious living occurs in spite of hurtful and stressful circumstances.

Victorious living can be a spiritual reality for those who are willing to be obedient to a life of prayerful discipleship and dependence on the Holy Spirit's work in their daily lives. In order to reach this state, we must understand the difference between contentment and happiness. Happiness is usually directly correlated with how well life is going at the moment, while contentment depends not on circumstances, but on God's ability to raise us above them and place us on solid, spiritual footing. It is on this solid footing that we can experience the work of the Holy Spirit in turning trials into glory. (See James 1:2.) Hope in the midst of hopelessness is impossible based on human strength alone, but it is possible when the supernatural blessing of God's grace and mercy provide the basis for victorious living.

These eleven principles have one common theme—the strengthening of faith and dependence on God. Coping with stressful situations requires that we develop a strategy in order to be successful. The Christian is compelled to strengthen the spiritual foundation of his life as the primary factor in developing an effective strategy that insures victorious living in spite of the circumstances.

CHAPTER 10

HELPING THE FINANCIALLY NEEDY

M erriam-Webster's Collegiate Dictionary (9th ed.) defines *benevolence* as "a disposition to do good, an act of kindness, a generous gift."[1] Solomon taught, "Whoever is kind to the needy honors God" (Prov. 14:31, NIV), and "Blessed are those who help the poor."(Prov. 14:21) Also, Acts 6:1 and 1 Timothy 5:3 give evidence that the early church provided for the care of the widows among them. This disposition to do good and to act with kindness should be a natural response of the church as it ministers to the needs of its people and reflects the love of Christ. Meeting the material needs of the poor is a point of contact through which effective and strategic ministry can flow. In a tangible, practical, and observable way, benevolence communicates not only the love of Christ, but also His presence in the moment of need or crisis.

Helping people who are in financial crisis establishes a bond of appreciation and caring between the individuals and the church that is powerful and long lasting. It also establishes an identity that is positive and genuine for the church in the community. When we as a church care for the financially needy in our community, we are literally putting our money where our mouth is. Those on the outside looking in long to see genuineness and authenticity in the way we conduct ourselves based on our biblical worldview and relationship to Jesus Christ. A woman who had just been given a car by our benevolence ministry told us that her unchurched boss was astounded that anyone would be that generous. He even offered to drive her to the church to pick up her new car so he could see for himself what had been given to her. What he saw made such a positive impression on him that he had to "check us out" and attended a Sunday service soon thereafter.

We have experienced the blessing of God in our benevolence ministry in powerful ways since we decided in the early 1980s to create a staff position to administer our program and develop consistent application of our guidelines for helping the needy. The program has grown from a modest beginning to the point that we give away over two hundred sixty thousand dollars annually to individuals and families in financial crisis. In addition to money used to pay for living expenses, we maintain a food closet and a car ministry that provides much-needed transportation for about thirty families each year.

The Casas Benevolence Ministry is funded from the annual church budget (20 percent), designated gifts (68 percent), and special offerings (12 percent). The benevolence fund is now the third largest designated fund in our church budget, following only the building and missions funds. Benevolence has become one of the primary distinctives of our church's image in the community. The growth in giving to this ministry is directly linked to the number of people who were at one time helped financially themselves and now give generously each year because of the impact of the ministry on their own lives. It is a ministry that has literally generated its own support base and established its viability and permanence as a vital part of the overall mission of the church. In the ten-year period from 1994 to 2003, this fund grew from $45,696 a year to $240,929—an 81 percent increase. During those ten years, $1,553,737 was given to needy people. Budgeted funds amounted to $310,747 and designated giving equaled $1,056,561. An additional $186,448 was received from special offerings.

Most churches fund the benevolence ministry as a budget line item and may supplement it from designated giving including special offerings. In our case funding from the budget alone proved to be inadequate to meet the needs of the congregation. Establishing a budget line item has the advantage of providing a foundation upon which to build a strong benevolence ministry. A church budget should contain funds for helping the financially needy as one of the ways the biblical mandate for helping the poor can be carried out. As budgets are developed each year, the inclusion of funds for benevolence reinforces this responsibility in the minds of the congregation. Funding a benevolence account also lets the community know the church is serious about helping the poor. Budgeting funds also prevents a "management by crisis" approach to helping people that arises when there are no monies to meet a need.

The other two primary methods of funding also have their advantages and disadvantages. Designated giving on a consistent basis does increase the church's ability to help more people and to be more responsive to crises when they arise. Special offerings can be effective in meeting a specific one-time need, like helping a family whose house burned down or providing funds for unusual medical bills. We primarily use special offerings to keep the benevolence fund at a certain level to insure its consistency and availability. The major disadvantage in using special offerings or asking for donations to the benevolence fund is that it may become counterproductive if it occurs too often. Frequent requests can be seen as a crisis management approach to dealing with the needs of the poor. At Casas we use all three funding sources to ensure we have the funds available to consistently meet the needs of our congregation and community.

We have established a policy that our church families will be served first if funding is tight. Of course we want to avoid being in this position, and utilize the combination of all three funding sources to fully meet the needs. It is also important to note that 100 percent of the funds given to the benevolence ministry from any source goes to help those in financial need. The personnel needed to administer this ministry are funded from the personnel line of the church budget rather than from the benevolence fund. By adequate staffing, well-defined policies and procedures, and consistent efforts to practice good stewardship, our benevolence ministry has prospered and outgrown our expectations. The giftings, abilities, and commitment to be good stewards on the part of our capable benevolence counselors has been the most important determinant in the success of our benevolence ministry. When both those being served and those who give the money to fund the ministry realize that competency and good stewardship are the norms for how the program is administered, its future as a viable and significant ministry of the church is secure.

While we have benefited from having a specialist we call a benevolence counselor conduct this ministry, there are other models used by churches that are also effective. The committee-as-decision-maker approach involves having two or more people reviewing cases and dispersing funds. The advantage this approach affords is that it tends to balance out the subjective biases inherently present when only one person is making the decisions. Its major drawbacks are that decision making is slower and the client may be intimidated by having to appear before a committee to present their needs or by having their needs and personal financial information reviewed in writing by a committee. This model has an institutional feel and may not communicate the same level of caring and personal regard that a benevolence counselor often does.

The minister-as-decision-maker approach is common among smaller churches. It has the advantage of being effective in keeping the minister in touch with the needs of his congregation as well as the community at large. It also allows for people in need to connect with the pastor on a personal level. This approach is limited by the amount of time the minister has to carefully evaluate each request and keep up with the availability of community resources. Busy pastors are also more vulnerable to the "professional client" who "works" churches as his means of livelihood.

The benevolence counselor model is effective in that it takes the responsibility off busy pastors and staff members who usually have to handle benevolence requests and places it on a specialist instead. This specialist can take the time to carefully evaluate each case, administer policy consistently and maintain a good working relationship with community resources. The specialist model offers the further advantage of being able to select a person with the spiritual gifting and personality traits best suited to benevolence ministry. We have learned that discernment, rather than mercy, is the gifting that is most productive in this ministry. The ability to hold the line and say no to requests that are genuine needs because they do not meet the criteria for distribution is an important personality attribute for anyone serving in a benevolence ministry.

Those who administer the funds have the responsibility to insure that good stewardship is practiced. We have established definitive policy criteria for the counselor to adhere to in order to remove "gray areas." For example, we do not give cash to anyone. Instead, we require those needing help to bring in their bills and review their financial situation in detail with our benevolence counselor. We operate on the premise that it is important to help as many people as we can with the funds available. Therefore, providing financial help for a short period is the norm. There are unusual cases that require support over a longer length of time. Those cases are reviewed in consultation with the associate pastor for pastoral care, and a dollar limit is established for how much help will be available.

We also often place responsibility on the individual to meet certain conditions in order for help to continue beyond a one-time request. For example, a person might be asked to bring in her financial records and participate in a budget planning session. It might also be the case that a person would be asked to begin a job search if he was unemployed. In some cases, we have encouraged people to sell assets in order to provide needed funds or reduce debt. In recent years we have requested that clients attend a Crown Ministry class as a condition of receiving financial assistance. Philosophically we try to establish that benevolence ministry to an individual or family is something we do *with* them and not just *for* them. We believe they have a responsibility to learn and follow basic biblical guidelines regarding money management and we have the responsibility to teach them and guide them in addition to providing money to meet specific bills.

Regardless of which model of benevolence ministry is used, it is incumbent upon those administering and serving in this ministry to do so in dependence on God's wisdom. Spiritual discernment and revelation are needed to guide and direct each session with each person. Praying for and with the clients is an integral part of this ministry in keeping with the philosophy that benevolence is primarily pastoral and ministerial and not administrative. We try to keep in focus the needs of the total person as we address the financial needs. A financial crisis is often just a symptom of deeper issues in a person's life that need to be addressed through Christian counseling.

Referral to and consultation with our pastoral counseling staff has become an important part of the benevolence counselor's role as a helper. We have worked to develop a comprehensive strategy rather than applying a "Band-Aid" approach. We emphasize the need to assess the emotional, spiritual, and relational health of the individual as well as deal with the immediate financial crisis. This needs-assessment process might reveal some or all of the following:

1. A need for budget counseling
2. A referral to our Crown Ministry program for the needed biblical education on how money is to be managed
3. A referral for marriage and family counseling
4. A need for career reevaluation
5. A need for legal advice
6. A need for medical care and evaluation
7. A need for connectedness to the Christian community through a Bible study or prayer group

8. A referral to our Celebrate Recovery ministry for a specific support or therapy group
9. A referral to our Freedom in Christ ministry

We have witnessed the healing that can occur in a church community with caring people. The church is clearly called and commanded to minister in a comprehensive way to the total person. The size of the individual church is not the determining factor in the effectiveness of ministering to the presenting financial needs and recognizing the systemic relationship to other areas of need in a person's life. A small church can be just as effective as a large one if it has developed a network of referral sources that include: Christian counselors, legal counsel, financial planning and budgeting, career planning, and job search. Ministries like Crown Ministries, Celebrate Recovery, Grief Care, Divorce Care, marriage enrichment and parenting skills, and ministries specific to single parents may also be available in cooperation with other area churches.

At Casas, our goal in ministries of all kinds is to think globally. We strive to see each need for ministry in whatever context as a "window of opportunity" to address the total person and his needs by encouraging a connection to the body of Christ. It is this connection that provides for the growth and healing so needed in every life. Through such connections, the church becomes personally alive to the individual as a living, functioning, spiritually and relationally powerful extension of Christ's ministry on Earth.

CHAPTER 11

TAKING CARE OF YOURSELF

In restoring others to health by healing their wounds, he must not disregard his own health and develop tumours of pride. Let him not, which helping his neighbours, neglect himself, let him not, which lifting up others, fall himself.

—St. Gregory, AD 591[1]

Ministering to the needs of others and managing the stress such ministry produces has been and will continue to be a major factor in the life of every pastor. Pastors have a responsibility to take care of themselves emotionally and physically as well as spiritually. Our experience of counseling many pastors over the years has revealed that most have been neglectful of their own emotional and physical health. Consider the case of Ned as illustrative of the experience of many pastors.

Ned's friend, a fellow pastor, suggested that he seek counseling to address the depression and discouragement he had been trying to handle himself. Ned took his first full-time pastorate upon graduation from seminary. He served three churches during his eighteen years in the ministry. He had been at his current church for seven years and had not seen the growth he thought would result from his leadership. Ned, like so many pastors, had a strong work ethic and put his whole life into his ministry. He was counseled by an older pastor to "devote 100 percent of your energy for the sake of the kingdom." He did just that and also expected his wife and family to do likewise. Ned reported that he worked seventy to eighty hours per week on average. He did take a two-week vacation every year. Ned's children reported that they have had many vacations interrupted by phone calls and he sometimes had to return to do a funeral or deal with a crisis. His wife said that when they go out together for a "date" he often scheduled a hospital visit on the way and that their conversation usually centered on church-related issues and people.

Ned allowed the expectations of others to define his job description and lived under the assumption that his job was conditional upon his meeting those expectations. Ned had few close friends and had not allowed himself to be vulnerable to other men in the church. This was due to an incident in which he shared with someone he trusted a confidence and was betrayed. His health was impacted by a lack of exercise, weight gain, and high blood pressure. He also recently dealt with a difficult relationship with his minister of education, who resigned under suspicion of misusing church funds. Ned expressed discouragement over the level of apathy he observed in his congregation and his inability to lead them out of it. He also mentioned that he had been discerning a level of spiritual interference in his ministry that he had not previously experienced.

Like most pastors, Ned attended seminars, retreats, and workshops on the topic of how to deal with stress in the ministry. However, he had not been able to avoid the depression that set in, even though he realized it was limiting his ability to apply what he knew would be of help to his own life. He needed the help of someone else who could provide a "safe" place in which to openly process his feelings about his life and ministry. Ned recognized he could not be effective trying to minister alone. He needed to be connected to others in a context in which he could be himself and not be viewed as the pastor.

We have addressed these issues that Ned faced many times over the years with our staff and have benefited from the wealth of resources available to help those in ministry cope effectively with the unique stressors inherent in the nature of the work. It seems that every ministry position carries with it a stress level that at some point must be dealt with if the individual is to be effective and productive. Based on my observation, the role of senior pastor is one of the most stressful professional positions in our society. Indeed from a historical perspective, it may always have been that way. One study revealed that 75 percent of pastors had a stress-related crisis at least once in their ministry.[2] Another survey reported 45 percent of pastors say they have experienced depression or burnout to the extent they needed to take a leave of absence from ministry.[3] A study on stress in the ministry reported most pastors see church politics, financial shortfall, and difficult staff and board relationships as the top three stressors in their lives.[4]

From our counseling experience, we have identified seven distinctives that set the pastorate apart as unique among professions.

The responsibility of "rightly dividing the word of truth" (2 Tim. 2:15, KJV) is just short of awesome and overwhelming. The importance of the responsibility is clarified when one considers the powerful influence a pastor has over the lives of people. Responsible, humble pastors feel the weight of this part of ministry as they prepare sermons and lessons that challenge and reach a wide range of biblical knowledge and understanding in their congregations. The weekly stress of being prepared sometimes for two or three different messages is compounded by the wide range of Christian maturity present in all congregations.

Pastoring requires the application of multiple skill sets. How many other professions require skillful performance in administration, human resources, financial planning and budgeting, counseling, teaching, preaching, and leadership, as well as the ability to communicate caring and compassion to a diversity of personalities and personal needs? It is not surprising to learn that 90 percent of pastors feel they are inadequately trained to cope with the diversity of demands in ministry and 50 percent said they felt unable to meet the needs of their jobs.[5] A distinctive component of the stress imposed by the requirement to possess multiple skill sets is the expectation of those served for expertise and competence in all of the dimensions of the job. The constant shifting of emotional and intellectual gears to accommodate the demands and expectations placed on the pastor is a constant stressor.

The high profile position of pastor in the natural realm is mirrored in the spiritual. The pastor is a main target of the enemy's attacks on the kingdom of God. Pastors who recognize this reality and develop strategies to deal with it reduce the stress incurred significantly. At Casas, our senior pastor and his family have the prayer cover of seventy praying men who receive from him and his wife specific requests and needs to bring before the Lord. Adequate prayer cover provides not only the spiritual support and protection needed by every pastor, but it also communicates strong emotional and relational support as well.

Pastors must deal with high expectations for performance both professionally and personally. Their lives are under constant examination and subject to critique and analysis by everyone including many outside the church. However, because pastors are human and possess weaknesses professionally and personally, there is a built-in tension between the expectations for near perfection and the reality of the limitations naturally in place in the life of every pastor. The feeling that "I live in a glass house" is common for most pastors. The reality of living life under constant examination by those served is seen by 80 percent of those in pastoral ministry as affecting their families in negative ways. The same study reported that 52 percent of pastors and wives believe that being in pastoral ministry is hazardous to their family's well-being and health.[6] A study by the pastoral ministries department of Focus on the Family revealed that 66 percent of pastors and their families feel pressure to model the ideal family to their congregations and communities.[7] Perhaps athletic coaches in major sports come close to the level of high performance expectations pastors face, but unlike pastors, they don't seem to face the same level of scrutiny imposed on their wives and children.

Pastors face financial stress due to inadequate salaries. Twenty-eight percent of pastors in one survey indicated their compensation was inadequate. Wives are often compelled by financial pressure to work outside the home. One study revealed that 58 percent of pastors' wives were employed.[8] Pastors are, when compared to other professions with similar educational requirements, significantly underpaid. The financial stress created by lower salaries is generally not recognized by the congregation, who assumes their pastor is willing to and should sacrifice materially, even though they themselves do not.

The "on call" nature of ministry results in the pastor never being able to get away from the stress of the job. Most pastors assume it is their duty to be available to the congregation at all times. It has been my observation that most pastors and their families do not benefit from a day off each week like most other employees enjoy. The concept of a "Sabbath day of rest" is foreign to most in church ministry. A leadership journal survey revealed 40 percent of pastors say they work more hours each week than they did five years ago.[9] The stress this creates on the emotional, physical, and relational health of the pastor and his wife can be very damaging. Eighty-one percent of pastors surveyed indicated that inadequate time with their spouse was a major stressor in their marriage.[10] In a more recent survey, pastors' wives described their husband's work schedule as a source of conflict in their marriage.[11]

Loneliness and isolation are common stressors in ministry. Save America reports 70 percent of pastors in their survey indicated they do not have someone they consider a close friend.[12] In a study conducted by *Leadership* magazine, 55 percent of pastors reported that they have no one with whom they can discuss their sexual temptations. Another study reported that 20 percent of pastors indicated they would go to no one for counseling and another 50 percent said they would seek help from another pastor.[13] The leadership role of the pastor is a lonely one primarily because of the expectations of others (and sometimes those of the pastor himself) that he be strongly self-sufficient, self-assured, and on top of his own issues. Many congregants seem to live vicariously off of the strength of the pastor and truly expect him to have such a powerful relationship with God that he doesn't need anyone but Him. In our years of ministry to hurting pastors, we have found that often the pastor himself comes to believe this notion and therefore chooses to function quite independently of accountable and healthy relationships with others. Many pastors who preach the need for connectedness in community with others find it difficult to establish personal relationships that are authentically honest and safe for them. Perhaps this loneliness and isolation is a contributing factor to inappropriate relationships. It has been reported that 20 percent of pastors say they view pornography at least once per month. Another 20 percent say they have had an affair while in the ministry. Approximately 20 percent of the calls received by the pastoral ministry department of Focus on the Family deal with sexual misconduct and pornography.[14]

In light of the existence of these seven stressors in the lives of those in ministry, we have over the years developed strategies to help our own staff and other ministers deal effectively with them.

Teaching and preaching

We have reorganized our church structure and the job descriptions to accommodate the need for the senior pastor and the associate senior pastor to have adequate time to prepare for their Sunday preaching assignments. Limiting the time spent in meetings has helped to preserve energy and time for our senior pastor. Based on our experience, we have taken steps to organize around strengths and to thereby maximize effectiveness and empower the natural gifting and abilities of those responsible for teaching and preaching.

Multiple skill set demands

We have hired ministers to address weakness and complement existing strengths. We know that one person cannot be expected to have high performance skill sets in all areas. Therefore we have made it our practice to hire individuals who are qualified and skilled in the area we needed to address. In the early years of our rapid growth, lay leadership was used to complement our strengths and minimize our weaknesses.

Dealing with spiritual attacks

We have educated our staff on spiritual warfare and helped them to face the reality of the spiritual battles inherent in doing kingdom work. We have tried to remain alert and listen to our prayer warriors when they discern attacks against individuals or ministry areas. Focused staff prayer meetings have been effective in keeping us on our toes spiritually, and helpful in dealing with oppression and specific enemy attacks.

Coping with high expectations

We have developed an accountability to others that helps our pastors stay on track with what each is called and gifted to do. Each minister has a supervisor to whom he or she is accountable. Job performance standards are established and expectations clarified. For example, ministers are required to work fifty-hour work weeks, and also to take at least one full day off each week. Time sheets are maintained and reviewed by supervisors to insure that the required time off is taken. Expectations for spouse's involvement in ministry are clarified during the hiring process. Preserving family time and encouraging healthy marital relationships are the norm for us. A liberal vacation policy of one month per year along with providing comp time for weeks that exceed fifty hours has been invaluable in reducing stress and preserving family time. Professional development is encouraged through the provision of ten days of conference time each year. Our sick leave accrues at the rate of one day per month with a ceiling of thirty-six days maximum. An additional blessing has been a month's sabbatical every five years, which has insured the healthy longevity of minister effectiveness. The expectations for job performance and availability are established and evaluated by the leadership of Casas, not by the immediate needs or demands of any member of the congregation.

Financial needs
We have benefited from an attitude on the part of leadership that we want to provide as much salary and benefits as is possible to our ministerial staff. Adequate compensation and benefits have reduced the level of financial stress for our staff. It is assumed that all of us could earn a higher salary in the corporate sector. Thus one of the conditions of employment we address with prospective employees is that, while the church will do the very best it can to provide adequate financial support, it will not be at the level of comparable employment elsewhere.

Being on call
We realized that as the church grew in size, the senior pastor could not cover all of the hospital visits, conduct all of the weddings and funerals, and be available for the urgent counseling requests. We developed a pastor-on-call program in which each minister takes a turn at being on call for a twenty-four-hour period. Ministers also share in the responsibility of covering funerals and weddings. The pressure on those who do the preaching and hence are the ones most likely to be expected to be "available" for everything from

walk-in counseling to being at the hospital at 5:30 a.m. to pray with someone before surgery thereby is reduced, if not eliminated.

Loneliness and isolation

One of the many advantages of serving on a staff of more than one pastor is the experience of sharing the joys and challenges of ministry with someone else who understands. Sharing with each other on retreats, in staff meetings, as prayer partners, and privately one to one has been healthy. Pastors who work and serve as the only staff member of their church must develop relationships with other pastors in their community if they are to benefit from the fellowship and accountability afforded in relationship with others.

Most pastors have been at least somewhat exposed to the wealth of information that exists regarding good stress management. One good example is *Stress Management for Dummies* by Allen Elkins. Another is *Stress Less* by Don Colbert. The work of Charles Figley in defining "compassion fatigue" as the unavoidable result of wearing effects of caregiving is a valuable resource for pastors.[15] Many pastors have attended seminars and workshops on this subject as well as read articles in periodicals coming across their desks. While this information is valuable and educational, its focus is most often on the symptoms of ministerial ineffectiveness rather than on the causes.

One causal factor that we have addressed in our ministry to hurting, stressed, and burned out pastors is the issue of individual woundedness. It has been our observation that individual woundedness, exacerbated by the stress of pastoral ministry, often leads to a breakdown of physical and emotional health. This results in increasing patterns of ineffectiveness in ministry and family life. The personal wounds carried by many pastors go unaddressed due to the focus on the demands of the ministry. As we have seen previously, individual woundedness is most often a result of abuse, abandonment, or neglect in childhood. Another cause of woundedness that should be considered is childhood trauma. The death of a parent or sibling; a serious illness of a parent, sibling, or self; accidents resulting in serious injury to family or self; and rejection by other children all leave their respective emotional wounds in the soul of the individual. Traumatic events in adulthood can also be a factor if they have not been dealt with in a healthy manner. The death of a child, divorce or death of a spouse, a serious illness, or accidents involving family are all devastating emotional events which leave deep wounds.

Many pastors have experienced the loss of a pastorate or have been betrayed by those they trusted and served. Experiencing events like these places enormous emotional stress on the person and their families. If left unresolved and unattended, these traumas can be manifested in symptoms such as:

- Addictive patterns with work, food, sex, alcohol, and drugs
- Marital conflict
- Depression and anger
- Anxiety and fear
- Rigidity and legalism
- Guilt and shame
- Low self-esteem
- Defensiveness and resistance to constructive criticism
- Unforgiveness and resentment
- Neglect of personal health
- Overextended view of self-importance

▶ Controlling, dictatorial behavior
▶ Physical health decline

At issue here is the tendency of many pastors to ignore these symptoms and therefore never address the probable causes of their own woundedness. If healing is to occur and ministry effectiveness to be restored, then a strategy of using the symptoms as indicators of woundedness and pursing them to get at the core issues is essential. Here are some practical suggestions to begin the healing process.

Commit to a process that may be time intensive and monetarily costly. Seek help from a Christian counselor who understands the role of the Holy Spirit in the healing process. Pursue inner healing with prayer teams and prayerfully attack areas of bondage and stronghold.

Examine your relationship with God and determine where the distortions exist. Pastors often spend so much time working for God that they neglect their own personal relationship with Him. It is assumed that religious activities like Bible study, prayer, worship, teaching, and preaching somehow equate with relationship. Busyness is one of the characteristics typically present in a pastor's life. It is often detrimental to spiritual and emotional growth. It can be a smoke screen masking the shallowness of one's relationship with God and a means of avoiding dealing with personal pain.

Set healthy boundaries within your ministry to protect and preserve the emotional and physical energy needed to address personal issues of woundedness. Give yourself permission to limit your workweek to fifty to fifty-five hours on average. Screen telephone calls using your secretary or the answering machine to insure you are in control of the time and method of response to the requests for your time. Take a full twenty-four-hour day off each week and schedule at least three weeks of vacation to be taken all at one time during the year. Protect your family time and place a priority on living outside of the "glass house" at least occasionally. Engage in activities that are non-ministry oriented.

Take care of your physical body. Join a gym and work with a fitness trainer to get a pattern of physical activity established. Perhaps churches should as a matter of course include a membership for a gym or health club as a part of the financial benefit package for their pastors. Eat a healthy diet and maintain a proper weight as determined by your physician. Get proper rest. Fatigue negatively impacts brain chemistry and therefore decreases one's ability to function efficiently and maintain good health.

Develop relationships with peers outside your own church. Many pastors have formed fellowship and support groups with other pastors who help to reduce the isolation of the ministry. This increases the possibility of establishing safe relationships in which a pastor can be himself and occasionally detach from his role persona.

These recommendations are by no means meant to be all-inclusive. They are however foundational in supporting the process of personal healing and providing for consistent effectiveness in one's family and ministerial life. By taking good care of himself and his family, a pastor can facilitate modeling the abundant life Jesus spoke of in John 10:10: "My purpose is to give them a rich and satisfying life." The pastors we have known and worked with are deeply committed to proclaiming the glorious message of the gospel to a needy world. They are willing to make personal sacrifices in order to do so. They feel a personal call to ministry and have great hearts of compassion for the needs of others.[16] They are truly special people being used by God for His kingdom work. May they all heed the advice of St. Gregory not to neglect their own needs and thereby limit or neutralize their ability to serve, lead, teach, and minister to God's children.

CHAPTER 12

TRENDS IN PASTORAL CARE

In chapter 1 we discussed the historical connection between the pastor of today and his counterparts of yesterday. We saw that "soul care" has been and will continue to be one of the primary functions of the pastorate. In this chapter, we will examine six trends that shape and direct our current efforts to be effective in caring for the souls of our people.

Recovery Ministries

We live in a culture that often seems to be dominated by addictive and compulsive behaviors related to food, sex, money, legal and illegal drugs, alcohol, work, television, relationships, hobbies, and materialism in general. It is a culture not unlike the ancient cultures surrounding the children of Israel in that our compulsions and addictive patterns lead us into the practice of idolatry. Idolatry is the core spiritual issue present in addictive behavior.

As churches, we have a responsibility to contribute to healthy recovery strategies by offering a biblical worldview perspective that addresses idolatry and the spiritual bondage it creates in the lives of people. Churches are recognizing the need to be a part of the recovery process and not just supportive bystanders. Recovery programs are now appearing in many churches as they strategically respond to the "tsunami" of addiction that is sweeping over the church in the twenty-first century. It is our opinion based on observation that recovery will be a focal point of "soul care" for the modern church in this century.

We are fortunate to have effective and proven approaches, models, and programs available to us. As previously discussed in chapter 7, Celebrate Recovery, developed by Saddleback Community Church, is the model Casas has chosen to help those caught in the web of addiction get free and maintain a healthy recovery. The National Association for Christian Recovery provides another resource through its publications, workshops, and conventions. Fuller Theological Seminary has established an Institute for Recovery Ministries and is offering a degree in Recovery Ministries to train ministers to help the many in our churches who have had to depend on secular programs for their recovery. The need is great and the challenge substantial, but the spiritual resources of the church are powerfully effective and more than adequate to meet the challenge.

As recovery ministries are established, it is important for the church to be prepared to meet the underlying causes of addictive behavior. In our experience, Twelve Step-based recovery ministries help to identify the emotional, relational, and spiritual woundedness of the individual, but often do not offer healing models to accompany the recovery programs. The church is uniquely empowered to offer healing and restoration as the Holy Spirit ministers to the wounded and frees the captives from spiritual bondage. We discussed in chapters 3, 4 and 7, how we have approached facilitating the work of the Holy Spirit in these areas. There is a need for strategic planning and program development if churches are to be effective in providing recovery options for the captives in our midst and if we are to assume our position as a primary resource for all who seek help in recovering from addiction.

Christian Counseling

Christian counseling will continue to emerge as a recognized and accepted "adjunct" in the mental health field. It is and will continue to be defined by educational, ethical, and credentialing standards under the guidance and direction of the American Association of Christian Counselors (AACC). The AACC has over fifty thousand members in the United States and other countries, and is the driving force pushing Christian counseling into "adulthood" in this decade of the twenty-first century. As Clinton states, "Professional Counselors are uniquely equipped and positioned to help the church achieve its mission to evangelize and disciple."[1] Do pastors and church leaders recognize the need for cooperation, interaction, and collaboration with Christian counselors? The AACC has been working to establish clear, mutually supportive, and mutually respected ties with local churches and local church leaders.[2] It is our observation that Christian counselors want to play a part in helping to strengthen the health and vitality of the local church. They want it be to be a holy, powerful, and radiant church that ministers with compassion to its wounded souls.

The AACC represents the heart of the professional Christian counselor in stating: "We want Christian Counselors to be a community of light, image bearers of the living God who radiate hope and deliverance to a jaded, sated and broken world."[3] Pastors are joining with Christian counselors under the AACC umbrella, some ten thousand of them to date, to continue the process of establishing mutually beneficial collaboration working toward the same spiritual goals. One area that will be the focus of some attention will be the relationship between the pastor, pastoral counselor, lay helpers, and the professional Christian counselor. Defining boundaries and roles, and bringing clarity to them will be accomplished in the continuing dialogue between these caregivers. Pastors and Christian counselors will be working together in the development of the following areas of interest:

1. A Christian counseling code of ethics that defines standards of care internationally

2. National credentialing standards, which will demonstrate some level of competence and fidelity to biblical principles

3. Accreditation standards for Christian graduate training programs

4. Doctoral-level programs for Christian counselors, which would provide training in Bible, theology, research, policy, the bio-psych-social-spiritual sciences, spiritual formation, and pastoral care

5. Increased focus on quality biblical and theological training for professional counselors with the expectation that interaction between the theologian

Bible teacher and the counselor will be challenging and beneficial to both

6. Intentionally working with faith-based initiatives to partner with the church to impact serving others in Christ's name. This partnership will increase the effectiveness of strategic community development interventions, resulting in people seeing Jesus as the church lives out His mission.

7. A heightened sensitivity to multicultural differences in ministry and to the diversity of cultures in our nation and within churches and denominations

The Christian counseling profession is in major transformation as a result of parallel changes in the church, the physical and mental healthcare field and the legal and regulatory environment. As Christian counseling continues to gain strength as a profession, it will exert more influence over how pastoral care is accomplished in the church. It will be the primary architect for shaping what pastoral care will look like in the future. The questions it poses will include: Are we prepared to address the hurts and needs of our church family? Do we rely too much on the cognitive as we seek to disciple believers? Are we aware of the emotional and spiritual roadblocks to Christian maturity that exist in the lives of our people? Are we better at being the spiritual school than we are at being the spiritual hospital? Do we recognize that making disciples means helping people to experience healing and wholeness in the broken places in their lives? Do we embrace a definition of making disciples that incorporates "healing of the soul" as equal in value and importance to Bible knowledge?

As these questions are addressed in a cooperative and collaborative partnership, the effectiveness of the ministry of the church will be increased to the benefit of the pastor, the counselor, and those they seek to help. The professional Christian counselor will also benefit from this partnership in that he will be held accountable to apply the truth of Scripture to the human condition of suffering with accuracy and integrity. Christian counselors will benefit from the church's influence to realize that the work of "soul care" is more about spiritual formation and discipleship than it is about psychotherapy or applying psychological principles. The Christian counselor cannot function effectively as a Christian helper without being connected to a local church and accountable to her. Gary Collins states: "Counseling is not Christian when it ignores the church and when it is done in isolation from the community of believers—who come together for the purpose of worship, edification, transformation and service."[4]

The professional Christian counselor needs to be a part of a local church's ministry and under the influence of the Holy Spirit as he or she works in the body of believers. This connection helps one to keep the preeminence of Jesus Christ at the forefront of their personal and professional lives. Christian counselors who see themselves as facilitators of the work of the Holy Spirit will be strong and effective partners with pastors. One preaches and teaches the Word and the other works on helping apply and integrate biblical truths into individual lives. In our experience at Casas Church, the close working relationship between the pastor and the counselor has been the most influential factor in determining the effectiveness of soul care in our congregation.

A working partnership was developed based on mutual respect and a desire to learn from each other. A shared belief that the local church is responsible to help hurting people experience healing and wholeness provides a strong foundation of cooperation and collaboration insuring the effectiveness and spiritual vitality of soul care ministry at Casas. Perhaps Isaiah 61:1–2 best captures the biblical essence of our common calling and defines this mutually responsible partnership between pastor and counselor. "The spirit of the Sovereign LORD is upon me, for the LORD has anointed me to bring good news to the poor. He has sent me to comfort the brokenhearted and to proclaim that captives will be released and prisoners freed. He has sent me to tell those who mourn that the time of the LORD's favor has come."

Spiritual Formation

There exists a considerable body of knowledge and literature on the subject of spiritual growth and formation with which most pastors are familiar. Writers like Thomas, Tan and Gregg, Moon, Whitney, and provide a wealth of resources and impetus to carefully examine how Christian counseling as it is currently practiced converges with the application of spiritual disciplines as they are understood biblically and historically. Hindson, Ohlschlager, and Clinton state: "Competent Christian counselors should be familiar with an array of spiritual formation strategies that can be taught to clients as the means to spiritual maturity and intimacy with God."[5] Tan agrees that teaching and encouraging clients to learn and practice the spiritual disciplines is the point of integration of biblical and spiritual practices into counseling.[6] Moon asserts that the inclusion of spiritual formation in counseling is the practice of "clinical theology." The pastor and counselor meet at this point in the life of the individual; one as teacher, and the other as mentor, discipler, and director.

The health of this process requires that both pastor and counselor understand and apply a relational perspective as intimacy with God increases and not just a set of homework activities like Bible study, prayer, worship, solitude, confession, simplicity, community, and service. The process as we understand it is at its core knowing God intimately, becoming more like Jesus Christ, and experiencing the flow of the Holy Spirit in one's life. We can anticipate that the pastor and the counselor will continue to partner to learn how to bring the uniqueness of their two roles together for the spiritual benefit of the individual. It is encouraging and promising to note that Ashland Theological Seminary is offering degree programs at the doctoral level in spiritual formation. Columbia Biblical Seminary offers a master's. degree in pastoral counseling and spiritual formation. Educational support for this process of integration and convergence will only accelerate its development. Pastors and counselors will be challenged to work and learn together as this process evolves.

Lay Helping Ministries

Many observers predict we are on the verge of an explosion of lay helping ministries within the church. Larry Crabb proposes that the deep wounds of the soul can be healed in the context of biblically-based church communities where deep personal relationships can be developed.[7] Siang-Yang-Tan believes that due to the growth of managed healthcare, many will be without coverage for mental health services and will therefore seek help from their churches and trained lay helpers who can provide service at no cost.[8] Dr. Tan also suggests that we will see lay helping approaches, include healing and deliverance ministries, as well as peer-helping ministries. Worthington predicts lay counseling will grow dramatically in the future, due in large part to the inability of professional counselors to keep up with the demand. He further suggests that more people will seek help from church-based counseling centers.[9]

Legal and ethical issues like confidentiality, competence, client choice, and supervision must be carefully considered by the church. Protecting the church by minimizing liability risk should be the guiding factor in establishing specific policies as lay helping ministries are developed and implemented. We have experienced difficulty at Casas in maintaining lay counseling ministries, primarily because of the existence of our professional counseling staff. We trained lay counselors to work in concert with our professional staff in the early 1980s, and then established a Stephen's Ministry in the 1990s. In both cases, the ministries could not be sustained over more than a three-year period. We identified two contributing factors for a lack of success. The first was a lack of potential counselor recruits to sustain the programs, and the second was the lack of a consistent client base. We were surprised by the decline in the number of potential recruits for the lay counseling programs. Once the initial group was trained and served a two-year commitment, each succeeding class of recruits was smaller until we reached a point that no one signed up for the training classes.

We also assumed the Lay Counselor/Stephen Minister would receive referrals from the professional counseling staff, augmenting the counseling process by providing individual support and care beyond the sessions with the professional counselor. While there were some clients who benefited from this opportunity, there were not enough to keep the program alive and effective. The professional counselor-client relationship was sufficient to meet the needs for connection and support for most people. So instead of being an ancillary to the process, the lay counselor was an addendum. People chose to work with the professional and did not see the lay counselor as a necessary part of their support system. The lack of a demand then discouraged the recruitment process and resulted in the decline of response to join training classes. In our case, the support groups and sponsors for individuals provided through the Celebrate Recovery program have seemingly met the need for connection and support for many counseling clients.

Neurobiology and Brain Science

Science stands on the verge of major breakthroughs in understanding how the brain works and how to treat dysfunctions in brain chemistry. The mapping of the brain and the human genome is described as one of the most exciting developments of our time in medicine and mental health.[10] Dr. Michael Lyles describes this development as, "Having as much impact on medicine and the human sciences worldwide as the Manhattan Project had on physics and international relations in the 1940s." "The difference between twentieth-century medicine and twenty-first century genome and proteome-based medicine will be as great as, if not greater than, the difference between medieval and modern medicine."[11] The potential to relieve human suffering by developing effective treatment strategies based on a greater understanding of the causes of mental illness this research is producing seems to be tremendous. Dr. Andreasen writes in her book *The Brave New Brain* that we are in "the golden age of neuroscience and its goal is to find a penicillin for mental illness."[12]

The powerful tools now being used by researchers include molecular genetics, molecular biology, neurobiology, and neuroimaging. Researchers in these areas are working cooperatively to increase their knowledge and understanding of how the brain, DNA, and genes work. Can we look forward to a time when the millions of people who suffer from mental illness will have medication that will allow them to participate in healthy living? Scientists agree that it will occur. The people we minister to spiritually and emotionally in the church will have an opportunity to grow spiritually and develop healthy relationships without the albatross of mental illness weighing them down. Dr. Amen states, "The brain needs a healthy soul and the soul needs a healthy brain."[13] People who suffer from the four major groups of mental illness—schizophrenia, dementia, mood disorders, and anxiety disorders—will have relief. Significant numbers of Christians will be impacted. Consider that schizophrenia affects 1 percent of the population, manic-depression another 1 percent, major depression 10 percent to 20 percent, and Alzheimer's Disease 15 percent of people over sixty-five years of age.[14] Many of the people we have prayed for and supported and encouraged will be relieved of much of their suffering. While most of us as pastors, counselors, and church leaders would accept the notion that biology is not destiny, there will be challenges to theology and faith from the interpretation of what these new discoveries mean to the general population. Is, for example, our behavior determined by brain function rather than individual choice? Are sinful thoughts and behaviors a result of "biology"? Is there a gene that predisposes one to be more religious than another? Is anxiety and worry a lack of faith or the result of brain chemistry?

Pastors will benefit by being informed regarding the scientific discoveries in brain mapping and genome mapping as they occur so they can be ready to help interpret them theologically. Hopefully theologians and the church will play a role in giving direction to the development of ethical guidelines that will become necessary as new knowledge is acquired and genetic engineering techniques are developed. Dr. Worthington believes that many of the problems brought to pastors and counselors by clients in the years ahead will be bioethical issues, as people struggle with issues such as aging, dying, and pain management.[15]

Many exciting challenges lie ahead for those in the helping professions. May we look forward with optimism and faith as researchers reveal the complex and wondrous design of the Creator and join them in marveling at what God has created!

Professional Licensure, Risk Management, and Christian Counseling

Christian counselors, pastors, and church leaders have a dual responsibility. On one hand, they must follow biblical guidelines and meet biblical standards, and on the other they must meet the standards imposed by the courts and state licensure boards. At Casas, we have been careful to meet all of the professional standards of good mental health practice and to minimize liability risk by developing good risk management policies. For, example, our professional counseling staff has met all the state requirements for certification and licensure. We have established risk management procedures like the informed consent statement which all clients sign, maintaining clear lines of separation between the counseling ministry and church discipline, and honoring the confidential nature of the counseling relationship. We have been careful never to intentionally violate dual-relationship guidelines. For example, our counselors would never enter into a business or social relationship with a client or church member that would compromise the dual-relationship standards adhered to by professional counselors.

There do remain, however, questions that we are currently in the process of answering. These questions are surfacing as a result of states moving from certification to much more demanding licensure laws. Christian counselors, especially those who work in church-based counseling ministries, are affected by more demanding standards and control exerted by state boards as they define the practice of counseling in their respective states.

The crucial question for Christian counselors and churches is to what extent state licensure boards will restrict the practice of counseling to their own definition. Will Christian counseling be seen as an acceptable adjunct to the practice of professional counseling? In Arizona, the statute defining counseling reads: "The professional application of mental health, psychological and human development theories, principles and techniques to: a. facilitate human development and adjustment throughout the life span. b. assess and facilitate career development. c. treat interpersonal relationship issues and nervous, mental and emotional disorders that are cognitive, affective or behavioral. d. manage symptoms of mental illness. e. assess, appraise, evaluate, diagnose and treat individual, couples, families and groups through the use of psychotherapy."[16]

Two questions immediately come to mind when reading this definition:

1. Do non-ordained (ordained clergy are exempt in Arizona from state licensure requirements), licensed professional counselors who employ a biblical worldview that includes the use of prayer, spiritual warfare concepts, and a belief in supernatural

healing, meet the state's definition of what a licensed counselor is and does?

2. Could the practice of Christian counseling as we understand it be interpreted as engaging in activities as a licensee that are unprofessional by current standards of practice?

As we consider these questions there are at least two approaches a church and Christian counselors can take. The first approach is to ordain counselors and define their roles as clergy who are helping hurting people in the context of the historical position of the church. The second approach is to meet all the standards of licensure and be prepared to defend the use of Christian beliefs as acceptable for the professional Christian counselor as a viable "adjunct technique." The backing of the American Association of Christian Counselors will go a long way toward helping to establish an acceptable position for Christian counseling to occupy in the mental health field.

The AACC has established the American Board of Christian Counseling, whose mission is to define Christian counseling within the framework of its ties to the psycho-bio and social fields of study and research. The results of this group's work will provide us all with guidance and direction as we establish the legitimacy of our position in the mental health field and also in the eyes of the states and the courts.

We should approach the future of our relationship with state licensure boards and to how the courts might view our work as Christian counselors with confidence and faith. The AACC's code of ethics, section ES5-410, defines a biblical position from which we can operate and develop our strategy for dealing with potential conflicts and challenges: "Christian Counselors are bound to honor the law in every way possible. However, when the law is in direct opposition to God, and if unable to harmonize the mandates of scripture and the law, we declare and support the right of Christian Counselors to elect judicious non-adherence to those ways that offend the way of Christ."[17]

In spite of the great advances in science and technology that we can anticipate in the future, the pastor and the counselor will continue to deal with the unchangeable issues that plague the human condition. Issues like marital conflict and dissatisfaction, grief and loss, addictions, chronic emotional and physical pain, and the ultimate question, "Where is God in the midst of my suffering?" will remain the focus of pastoral care in the next generation just as they have for each previous generation. We can be assured the next generation of pastors and counselors will minister with greater knowledge and understanding. Let us pray they will do so with humility and sensitivity to the leading of the Holy Spirit.

NON-CHRISTIAN SPIRITUAL EXPERIENCE INVENTORY

(Mark all that apply)

Occult (Entry Level)

Astrology/horoscope
Automatic writing
Card laying
Crystals
Crystal ball
Edgar Cayce
ESP
Fetishism
Fortune telling
Handwriting analysis

Kabbalah/cabala
Levitation (light as a
feather)
Magic charming
Magic eight ball
Nostradamus
Ouija board
Palm reading
Psychic reading
Rod and pendulum

Self-hypnosis
Self-realization
Table lifting
Tarot cards
Tea leaves
Telepathy/swapping
minds
UFOs/alien abduction
Visualization

Occult (Severe)

Astral projection
Black and white
magic
Channeling
Clairvoyance
Divination
Dungeons and
dragons

Harry Potter
Hypnotism
Materialization
Mystical meditation
Séance
Shamanism
Sorcery
Speaking in a trance

Spiritualism/spiritism
Spirit guide/
imaginary friend
Transcendental
meditation
Vampirism
Voodoo/Santeria
Witchcraft/wicca

(continued on next page)

New Age Teachings

A Course in Miracles
Angels
  (communicating
  and worshiping)
Deepak Chopra
Eckankar
Embraced by the
  Light
Feng shui
Forum Landmark (pre
  1999)
Lifespring

Martial arts
Metaphysics
Mind control
  philosophies
New Age
New Age corporate/
  occult training
Parapsychology
Ram Das
Reiki
Reincarnation
Rosicrucian

Roy Masters
Science of the mind
Science of creative
  intelligence
Scientology
Silva mind control
Sexual attitude
  reassessment
Swedenborgianism
Tai chi
Therapeutic touch
Yoga

Cults and False Religions

Branhamism (The
  Message Church)
Children of God
Christian science
Church of the Living
  Word
Father Divine
Islam
Native American
  religions
Jehovah's Witnesses

Mormonism
The Boston Church
The Unification
  Church
Unitarianism
Unity
United Pentecostal
  Church
Bahaism
Black Muslims
Hare Krishna

Hinduism
Universal Fellowship
  of Metropolitan
  Community Church
Zen Buddhism
  (Buddhism)
Freemasonry (De
  Molay, Eastern Star,
  Rainbow Girls, Job's
  Daughters, Shriners)

HAVE YOU EVER...

▸ Sought healing through magic, conjuration, charming, psychics, holism, New Age, or Native American methods?

▸ Entered into a blood pact with another person or cut yourself in a destructive way?

▸ Made a vow, covenant, or pact with any individual or group other than God? (An example might be a vow made in a sorority, fraternity, or an inner vow.)

▸ Watched horror movies that were disturbing to you?

▸ Been involved in Halloween activities?

▸ Been involved in heavy metal or allied kinds of rock music? Played occultic computer or video games?

▸ Had counseling that encouraged you to seek a spirit guide, or involved channeling, visualization, hypnosis, New Age techniques, or anything that you felt concerned with?

▸ Tried to locate a missing person or object by consulting someone with psychic powers?

▶ Encountered ghosts or materializations of a person known to be dead?

▶ Read or possessed occult literature including the *Satanic Bible, Book of Shadows, Secrets of the Psalms, Sixth and Seventh Books of Moses,* and so on?

▶ Possessed occult or pagan religious objects that were made for use in pagan temples or religious rites, or in the practice of magic, sorcery, witchcraft, divination, or spiritualism?

▶ Been the object of a sexual attack by demons (incubi, succubi)?

▶ Been a victim of satanic ritual abuse or have you seen or been involved in satanic worship of any form?

▶ Had periods in childhood or in the present when you cannot remember what happened?

▶ Heard voices in your mind or had repeating and nagging thoughts condemning you, or that were foreign to what you believe or feel—like there was a dialogue going on in your head?

▶ Are there any other spiritual experiences you have had that would be considered out of the ordinary (such as sensing an evil presence in your room at night)?[1]

APPENDIX C

THE INDICATORS OF DEMONIC OPPRESSION AND ATTACK

▶ A family history of demonic influence coming from witchcraft, satanic worship, or Native American, New Age, Eastern religious practices, or Freemasonry.

▶ Disinterest in or the inability to read Scripture, comprehend the teaching of the Word, or participate in worship and prayer.

▶ Possession of items used in pagan, New Age, Eastern, or Native American worship rituals and Freemason ceremonies.

▶ Personal experience with any of the practices, cults, or religions listed on the Non-Christian Spiritual Experience Inventory.

▶ Fearful, bizarre dreams or night experiences related to sexual perversion, occultic symbolism, or violence. Evil presences, visitations, or impressions of demonic faces.

▶ Conscious invitation extended to Satan or demons to become involved in one's life.

- ▶ Systematic patterns of personal sinfulness such as lying, dishonesty, and resentment toward others, sexual acting out, and racial hatred.

- ▶ Personality disturbance, such as paranoia, vengefulness, physical, emotional, sexual, or spiritual abuse of others, self-mutilation, suicide attempts, depression, rebellion, and bizarre, violent, or blasphemous thoughts.

- ▶ Addictions to alcohol, drugs, sex, work, food, exercise, Internet, or television.

- ▶ Experiencing no relief from medical treatments (including drugs), personal prayer, Christian counseling, or biblical discipleship.

ROGER BARRIER SERMON NOTES

Dealing with the Devil

(Matthew 8:28–34); December 2, 2001

The story of Jesus' encounter with the two demoniacs from Gadera is a lovely presentation of Jesus Christ. (Read Mark 5:1–20 for the more detailed parallel account.) Again and again the compassion of Christ is displayed. Some hated these demoniacs. That is understandable. Some feared these demoniacs. That is understandable. Some did all they could to exterminate these demoniacs. That, too, may be understandable.

But as far as I can tell, the only person who loved the demoniacs was the Lord Jesus Christ. This is perfectly understandable in light of the character and compassionate heart of the Lord Jesus.

This morning I will use this passage as a touchstone to share a short primer on spiritual warfare. Several principles "jump out" at us as we examine this passage.

> When he arrived at the other side in the region of the Gadarenes, two demon-possessed men coming from the tombs met him. They were so violent that no one could pass that way.
>
> —MATTHEW 8:28, NIV

Demonization is real

Most spiritual attacks are not as dramatic as this one. However, over extended periods, less intensive attacks can be just as devastating. Subtle attacks often go undiagnosed and unrecognized.

We rarely consider that depression, despair, envy, anger, bitterness, jealousy, lust, deceit, or pride may have a spiritual warfare component. It is sad to watch folks struggle with their families, personal lives, or job situations and never consider that Satan is out to kill, steal, and destroy our joy, energy, abundance, jobs, families, and intimacy with God. (See John 10:10.)

> "What do you want with us, Son of God?" they shouted. "Have you come here to torture us before the appointed time?"
>
> —MATTHEW 8:29, NIV

Some problems can be understood only in light of satanic activity. Christians can never be demon possessed; however, they can be spiritually neutralized.

Christians need instruction concerning Satan's devices. First-century Christians had trouble recognizing Satan's attacks, and so do we. (See 2 Corinthains 2:11.)

Evangelism improves when we realize that many refuse Christ, not because they love their sin, but because Satan blinds their eyes so that they cannot see the gospel (See 2 Corinthians 4:3–4.)

Satan's major tool is deception. Job was deceived. (See Job 1:21; 2:10.) Since perfect Eve was deceived (2 Cor. 11:3), how vulnerable must we imperfect people be to misdiagnose his intentions? Or course, the very word *occult* means "hidden."

The Bible constantly warns Christians to beware of satanic harm. (See Acts 13:10; 2 Corinthains 11:13–15; 2 Thessalonians 2:9–12; 1 Timothy 4:1; 2 Timothy 3:13.) Satan's tools include: lying (John 8:32, 44), anger (Eph. 4:26–27), an unforgiving spirit (2 Cor. 2:10–11), sin (Eph. 2:1–2; 1 John 3:8–10), accusations and insinuations (Rev. 12:10), temptation (1 Cor. 7:5; 1 Thess. 3:5), contact with the occult (Deut. 18:10–13), and drug and alcohol abuse (Gal. 5:21).

Can a Christian be demon possessed?

We are careful never to use the term "demon possessed." In fact, the exact term "demon possession" is never found in the Greek Bible. The Greek word is actually *demonized*. The term *demonized* allows for different degrees of severity.

The battle is for the mind. Satan cannot completely destroy Christians. (See John 10:10; Acts 26:17–18; 1 Corinthains 3:16; 6:19–20; Ephesians 4:27; Colossians 1:13; 1 John 4:4.) But he can certainly wreak havoc in their lives (Eph. 6:12; 2 Tim. 2:24–26; 1 Pet. 5:8–9).

Since the earth is now in the hands of the evil one. (See Matthew 4:8–9; John 14:30–31; 16:11; 2 Corinthians 4:4; Ephesians 2:1–2; 1 John 5:19.) Christians are guerilla soldiers behind the enemy's spiritual lines. We must take care not to be taken captive and spiritually neutralized.

Careless Christians leave themselves open to satanic attack

The masquerading tools of the occult world surround us. I never cease to be amazed at unsuspecting Christians who use a demonic tool to open the door to the occult. Our deliverance ministry has a checklist of past activities for people to examine:

- ▸ Contact with occult activity (Deut. 18:9–13 is God's glossary of the occult)
- ▸ Personal invitation for demonic guidance and help (2 Cor. 11:4)
- ▸ Drug and alcohol involvement (Gal. 5:21)
- ▸ Perpetual sin (Eph. 4:27)
- ▸ Transference (Exod. 20:5–6)
- ▸ An undisciplined or "out of control" mind (2 Cor. 10:3–5)
- ▸ Sexual sin or abuse

> Some distance from them a large herd of pigs was feeding. The demons begged Jesus, "If you drive us out, send us into the herd of pigs." He said to them, "Go!" So they came out and went into the pigs, and the whole herd rushed down the steep bank into the lake and died in the water.
>
> —MATTHEW 8:30–32, NIV

God provides the necessary tools for victory over any demonic attack

Here is a spiritual warfare primer for handling a "satanic foothold" in our lives (Eph. 4:27). James 4:7 states: "Submit yourselves, then, to God. Resist the devil, and he will flee from you" (NIV). Submitting to God involves:

1. Confessing the area that is out of control

2. Consciously yielding the area to God

3. Considering self dead, according to Romans 6, to the sin in that area. If these three activities provide

freedom, then the problem was only a sin of the flesh. If the struggle continues, consider that this may be a spiritual attack. Proceed with the second half of James 4:7.

Resisting the devil deals with how we are to respond to attacking spiritual forces. Finding freedom involves:

1. Forsaking the sin so the forces of evil no longer have a foothold

2. Renouncing the attacking forces *(In the name of Jesus Christ, depart and leave me alone. I rebuke you and your attacks against me. I want nothing to do with you.)*

3. Asking for the filling of the Holy Spirit

4. Imploring the Holy Spirit to build a hedge of protection around you from future attacks, according to Job 1:10. The hedge is built according to Psalm 91.

It is easier to avoid a spiritual attack than to struggle through one later. Put on the Christian armor of Ephesians 6:10–17.

Understand that spiritual warfare and a demonic problem is always a prayer project.

Overcoming the devil is a must-learn skill in the process of spiritual growth. Remember, spiritual young men and women—not children—are the ones who have overcome the evil one (1 John 2:12–14).

Those tending the pigs ran off, went into the town and reported all this, including what had happened to the demon-possessed men. Then the whole town went out to meet Jesus. And when they saw him, they pleaded with him to leave their region.

—MATTHEW 8:33–34, NIV

Jesus inspires the most incredible reactions.

CASAS POLICY STATEMENT ON IDOLATRY

▶ We affirm that God established that His people are to have no other gods before Him, and are not to bow down to worship anything in any form (Exod. 20:3–4).

▶ We agree that idolatry is the replacement of God in the heart or mind of an individual by any material object, relationship, fleshly desire, false religion, or occultic practice. Idolatry results in bondage to the spirit of this world and diminishes the preeminent position of Jesus Christ as exalted by God to the highest place (Phil. 2:9).

▶ We identify the activities and groups listed in the Non-Christian Spiritual Experience Inventory as offering counterfeit religious experiences, false guidance, and diminishing and denying the preeminent position of Jesus Christ. We affirm that participation in, allegiance to, or experience with any of these activities or groups is idolatry and places an obstacle in our personal relationship with Christ.

▶ We acknowledge the need to confess sin and renounce participation in any activity or group that denies and compromises the preeminent position of Jesus Christ, offers guidance through any source other than the absolute authority of Scripture, or requires secret initiations, ceremonies, or covenants (1 John 1:5, 7). We urge any who have been involved in these to contact the Casas Adobes Baptist Church freedom ministry, which will facilitate God's work of healing, cleansing, and spiritual restoration in his or her life.[1]

SEVEN STEPS TO FREEDOM

Casas adopted the seven-step model in 1994. Developed by Dr. Neil Anderson, it is widely used in thousands of churches to help people experience freedom. Confession of sin (James 5:16) and renouncement of Satan (Prov. 28:13) are the two pillars of this approach. You will find the steps described in detail in *The Bondage Breaker* and *Discipleship Counseling*, both by Dr. Anderson.

Step 1: Overcoming False Guidance

This first step deals with any involvement with or exposure to, the occult, cults, and false religions. The checklist defines the activities, groups, and beliefs that are by their nature idolatry, and hold God's people in spiritual bondage.

Step 2: Overcoming Deception

This step helps us to determine how we may have been deceived by Satan, ourselves, and the world. The goal is to expose lies and affirm truth. A powerful "doctrinal affirmation" concludes the work in this step.

Step 3: Overcoming Bitterness

Forgiving those who have wronged us is basic to establishing a spiritually free life. Forgiveness is an act of obedience before God and prevents Satan from building a stronghold in our lives.

Step 4: Overcoming Rebellion

This step confronts defiance against authority and brings us to an understanding of biblical submission.

Step 5: Overcoming Pride

This step guides us to the acknowledgement of specific areas of personal pride. Confession and renouncement bring freedom from false humility and self-sufficiency.

Step 6: Overcoming Habitual Sin

This step helps us break the bondages of sin patterns in our lives. There are two sections to this step. One deals with the habitual sins of the flesh. The second section deals specifically with sexual sins.

Step 7: Overcoming Ancestral Sins

This step, based on Exodus 20:4–6, deals with the spiritual influence the sins of our ancestors can have on our lives. Curses are broken and freedom experienced in this important and often overlooked area.

CASAS STATEMENT ON HEALTHY LIVING: HEALING OUR DYSFUNCTIONS

▶ We are learning what the normal Christian life really looks like by healing misconceptions about God, the Bible, and by sorting out earlier misconstrued religious experiences.

▶ We are developing a culture of grace, openness, and vulnerability where we are genuinely open about weaknesses and mistakes.

▶ We are learning to handle conflict well by refusing to allow secrets, back-stabbing, and gossip, by handling criticism maturely, and by refusing to let conflict go underground.

▶ We are minimizing confusion and uncertainty by aligning ourselves around clear-cut priorities and objectives.

▶ We are emphasizing a culture of healthy relationships based on a biblical understanding of the true nature of man as both fallen and alone.[1]

BECAUSE GOD LOVES ME

1 Corinthians 13:4–8

▸ Because God loves me, He is slow to lose patience with me.

▸ Because God loves me, He takes the circumstances of my life and uses them in a constructive way for my growth.

▸ Because God loves me, He does not treat me as an object to be possessed and manipulated.

▸ Because God loves me, He does not need to impress me with how great and powerful He is because He is God; nor does He belittle me as His child in order to show me how important He is.

▸ Because God loves me, He is for me. He wants to see me mature and develop in His love.

▸ Because God loves me, He does not send down His wrath on every little mistake I make, of which there are many.

- Because God loves me, He does not keep score of all my sins and then beat me over the head with them whenever He gets the chance.

- Because God loves me, He is deeply grieved when I do not walk in the ways that please Him because He sees this as evidence that I don't trust Him and love Him as I should.

- Because God loves me, He rejoices when I experience His power and strength and stand up under the pressure of life for His name's sake.

- Because God loves me, He keeps on working patiently with me even when I feel like giving up and can't see why He doesn't give up on me too.

- Because God loves me, He keeps on trusting me when at times I don't even trust myself.

- Because God loves me, He never says there is no hope for me. Rather He patiently works with me, loves me, and disciplines me in such a way that it is hard for me to understand the depth of His concern for me.

- Because God loves me, He never forsakes me, even though many of my friends might.

- Because God loves me, He stands with me when I have reached the rock bottom of despair, when I see the real me and compare that with His righteousness, holiness, beauty, and love. It is at a moment like this that I can really believe that God loves me.

—DICK DICKSON[1]

PRINCIPLES FOR DEALING WITH UNCHANGEABLE FAMILY SITUATIONS

▸ Acknowledge that only God can change another person
Scripture: Zech. 3:4; 2 Cor. 3:18; 1 John 1:8–9

▸ Be accountable to others for how you respond to others
Scripture: Matt. 22:39; Luke 6:36; Rom. 12:17–20; Eph. 4:2–3

▸ Concentrate on what you can change—your thoughts, attitudes, and behaviors
Scripture: Eph. 4:3, 15–16, 24–27, 30–32; Eph. 5; Col. 3:12–17

▸ Pray specifically and in accordance with Scripture
Scripture: 1 Sam. 12:23; Prov. 8:34; Matt. 26:41; 1 Thess. 5:17

▸ Develop a strong inner life of devotion
Scripture: 1 Chron. 16:11; Ps. 57:1; 88:9; 119:48; Hos. 6:3; 1 Cor. 2:2; 1 Thess. 4:11

▸ Accept things as they are—you don't have to like them or understand them
Scripture: Rom. 12:12, 17–21; 1 Pet. 2:20

▸ Understand that suffering isn't bad—it just hurts
Scripture: Ps. 66:10–12; 68:19; 119:66–67; Eccles. 3:4; Rom. 8:28

▸ Stay connected to a Christian support system
Scripture: Rom. 12:10; Heb. 10:25

▸ Maintain self-control
Scripture: Prov. 25:28; Gal. 5:23; James 1:26

▸ Avoid "if only" thinking
Scripture: Matt. 6:25; 2 Cor. 10:5; Phil. 4:6; Heb. 13:21

▸ Be assertive in applying your strategy
Scripture: 1 Chron. 22:16; Gal. 6:9; James 1:22; 2:17; 1 John 3:18

CHAPTER SUMMARIES

CHAPTER 1
PASTORAL CARE IN
HISTORICAL PERSPECTIVE

The pastor of today is linked to the pastor of yesterday through the ministry of pastoral care or soul care, as it was called by the early church. People continue to need comfort in times of grief, guidance in times of confusion, direction in times of wandering, healing in times of suffering, reconciliation in times of conflict, and admonishment in times of disobedience. The two significant early works addressing the pastor's role as a caregiver are *Pastoral Care*, written in AD 590 by Gregory, a Benedictine monk who went on to be the Bishop of Rome, and *A Christian Directory*, written in 1665 by Richard Baxter, a Puritan pastor and scholar. Gregory's work became the primary source of defining what pastor care and soul care entailed for the parish priest or pastor for one thousand years of church history. J. I. Packer states that Baxter's *A Christian Directory* is "the fullest, most thorough, most profound treatment of Christian spirituality and standards that has ever been attempted by an English speaking evangelical author."[1] Baxter established for evangelicals the norm for our emphasis on marriage and family life. He framed for us the view that God made us to fulfill the two great commandments; to love Him and to love our neighbors as we love ourselves and that loving others must begin in the home.

In their book *Pastoral Care in Historical Perspective*, authors Clebsh and Jaekle identify four functions of "care of souls" that have been distinct and consistent throughout church history. Healing—the restoration of a person to a condition of wholeness; sustaining—helping a hurting person to endure; guiding—assisting perplexed persons to make confident choices; reconciling—man to man and man to God. Pastoral care today, like soul care of the past, remains a prime function of the pastorate.

CHAPTER 2
A CONTEMPORARY PERSPECTIVE:
THE CASAS STORY

The Casas story is unique in the sense it is a departure from the norm for both our denomination and most evangelical churches in general. It is a story of a spiritual pilgrimage for its staff and lay leadership. The counseling ministry has been the means by which Casas discovered that hurting people have a hunger to connect with God in the midst of their emotional and relational suffering. We received questions like: Does God heal people today? Could my emotional problems be influenced by the demonic? and, Can you help someone who was abused in a satanic cult? We discovered that when hurting people came to the "emergency room" of the "spiritual hospital," they assumed we would have biblically sound answers and strategies for how to help them get well. The challenge faced by our staff and others in the emerging field of Christian counseling was how to integrate our professional knowledge and training with our biblical understanding. The difficult questions clients brought to the counseling sessions were motivators to accelerate the integration process. The role of the Holy Spirit and the supernatural intervention of God in the lives of His people were areas in which our knowledge and experience was incomplete. We were blessed as a staff and lay leaders to work in a spiritually and intellectually free environment in which a process of investigation, questioning, and experimentation with our emerging new biblical worldview could take place. The leadership of Casas was in agreement that we wanted to be facilitators of bringing the authority of Jesus Christ to bear on the sufferings of His people and to rejoice in the healing and freedom experienced. This pilgrimage has defined who we are and revealed who God wanted us to be. It shaped our "spiritual DNA" and clearly focused our identity within our doctrinal tradition.

CHAPTER 3
AN INTEGRATIVE MODEL: HEALING PRAYER AND COUNSELING

As the counseling ministry developed and Casas grew, it became obvious that our knowledge and ability to address the woundedness of many hurting people at the level necessary was limited. The healing model described in this chapter was developed over a twenty-year period. It is still evolving and is "in process." It provides a framework for our comprehension of the "mystery of God" as He works in the lives of His people. We have identified three levels of healing that need to be addressed by the church.

The first level is foundational in that all need the healing touch of the salvation experience. We have all witnessed the life changes that occur when a person experiences Jesus Christ. Many have experienced healing and freedom from demonic oppression at the moment of salvation. The church has been effective in providing "community" in which needs for belonging, comfort, and love have been met. We observed that while many experienced healing at this level, others carried their woundedness into their Christian life.

A second level of needed healing was identified. At this level we saw a pronounced need for freedom from spiritual and emotional bondage. For example, we learned that a person who had experience with false religions or the occult needed something more than a Bible study and counseling to experience the healing they needed and requested. The methods used to minister at level two are strategically focused on spiritual and emotional bondage and dependant on the intervention of the Holy Spirit and the prayer support of caring helpers.

A third level of healing is needed for those who have experienced severe abuse and trauma. It is at this level we encounter the greatest degree of woundedness. The process at this level is difficult and slow. Their relationship with God and others is distorted and dysfunctional. The Holy Spirit is the only source of their healing and restoration. The methods used to facilitate the work of the Holy Spirit include: inner healing prayer, discipleship counseling, and deliverance prayer. Because the woundedness has occurred "in relationship" with others, healing in the context of relationship with caring helpers is essential.

CHAPTER 4
HELPING THOSE IN
SPIRITUAL BONDAGE

The Casas healing model assumes there are three fundamental diagnostic categories that must be considered in the process of helping hurting people. We acknowledge that a person's suffering could have medical, psychological, and spiritual causes. If it is determined that demonic oppression is a likely cause, then the seven-step model is used to help the person experience freedom. A case study is used to demonstrate how this process works. An apologetic for a spiritual warfare ministry in the church is presented. We acknowledge that it is the Holy Spirit that brings the authority of Jesus Christ to bear on the bondage of the enemy in a person's life. The resulting freedom is one of God's blessings to His hurting people. It has been our experience that when areas of bondage are released, the individual is then free to respond to and participate in the insight-cognitive oriented process of internalizing biblical truth and experiencing changes in attitude, behavior, values, and worldview.

CHAPTER 5
HELPING DIFFICULT PEOPLE

Pastors and lay leaders often encounter individuals that demand more time than others, present plethora of needs that they expect the church to meet, and don't seem to make much progress in taking responsibility for their own health and well-being. In this chapter I identify classifications of individuals who are difficult to work with at best and perhaps at worst, are people we cannot help to make significant changes in their lives. Four personality disorders (histrionic, dependent, anti-social and borderline) were selected for detailed examination because they are among the most commonly encountered in church ministry. Suggestions are presented on how to deal with each personality type. The challenge posed by these difficult personalities force pastors to weigh the duty of care issues they owe their congregations with the demands and often genuine needs of the difficult person. Guidelines are listed which provide pastors and lay leaders with an operational framework in which healthy ministry can occur.

CHAPTER 6
HELPING TROUBLED MARRIAGES

One of the most common requests for counseling received by pastors is for marriage counseling. Pastors and the couples they serve have at their disposal a plethora of resources to help marriages and families build and maintain healthy relationships. It would seem to the objective observer that marriage and family life in this generation should be healthier than previous generations due to the quality and quantity of helpful resources available to all who need them. The evidence, however, indicates otherwise. According to a Barna study, 27 percent of born-again Christians are or have previously been divorced compared to 24 percent of adults who are not born again. Pastors and their leadership have a duty of care to the couples in their churches to provide effective strategies for helping them deal with times of crisis in their marriages. It has been our observation that there are two basic classifications of marriages existing in our churches. One I have identified as the functional marriage and the other as the dysfunctional marriage. Descriptions of the symptoms that are presented by each of these classifications and the strategies most likely to be effective to help are discussed. We recognize that most of the programs offered by churches are ineffective in helping the dysfunctional marriage. These couples are at a high risk for divorce and require a different set of strategies to address their needs. If we are to be effective in addressing the high divorce rate among Christians, new approaches must be developed and implemented. I propose that dysfunctional marriages are composed of one and often two wounded individuals. An effective strategy is one that incorporates dealing with core issues of woundedness inherent in the lives of individuals. Suggestions are offered as to what constitutes an effective strategy. A case study is used to illustrate how this process of addressing individual woundedness is effective in healing troubled marriages.

CHAPTER 7
HELPING THE ADDICTED

The addicted person presents a challenge for most pastors and church leaders. First is the confusion on how to separate the sin from the sinner. Historically, the church has been ineffective in providing ministry to those caught in addiction because of strong, negative reactions toward the behaviors emanating from the addiction. Second is confusion on how to help those who ask for the church's intervention. In this chapter, I present an apologetic for church-sponsored recovery programs. I compare recovery to sanctification and propose that recovery programs are a good fit for the evangelical church. Recovery from addiction and sanctification both seek to move a person from a place of hiding from God to knowing Him and accepting His unconditional love. The church is perhaps the most powerful resource available to addicts. It provides by its nature and makeup the spiritual and human resources needed for healthy recovery. Churches that offer recovery programs communicate to addicts that they are accepting and safe. Addicts see themselves as the leper outcasts of society and will respond to churches that do not blame and shame them. At Casas we have adopted the Celebrate Recovery model, developed by Saddleback Community Church, to address the needs of the addict. I single out sexual addiction for special attention because of its pervasive presence in the church. Our healing model addresses the spiritual bondage component present in the life of the addict as essential for healthy recovery. We believe healing and recovery occur in the interaction of a willing, obedient, seeking soul with a caring community of fellow strugglers, empowered by the grace, mercy, and forgiveness of the Lord Jesus Christ.

CHAPTER 8
DEALING WITH DISTORTED
IMAGES OF GOD

We have learned that hurting people often struggle with a distorted image of God. A distorted image of God impacts a person's life in three primary ways:

1. It affects and determines the direction of spiritual growth.
2. It influences behavior toward church and expressions of worship.
3. It impacts self-image.

Distortions are created most commonly by how one was parented. Tragic life events and expectations of God's role in them are often the root cause of distortions. A third major contributor to a distorted image of God is negative, hurtful experiences with religion and churches. As a result of life, images of God are formed and can be described in four classic ways:

1. God is seen as an enforcer who will exact punishment for any wrongdoing.
2. God is seen as disapproving, rejecting, critical or perfectionistic.
3. God is perceived as distant, absent, or uncaring.
4. God is viewed as a tyrant whose main job is to make life miserable.

Indicators that a person may be struggling with a distorted image of God include:

- Asking why and where questions
- Fear and a lack of trust
- A lack of joy and gratitude.

Suggestions for helping those caught in the trap of a distorted image of God are discussed in this chapter and include:

- Building a relationship with a safe person
- Identifying the distortion
- Understanding the causes
- Connecting with the Christian community
- Choosing to do the hard work of applying truth about God as an act of obedience to Him.

The church has a responsibility to deal honestly with the issue of distorted images of God through its teaching and counseling ministries.

CHAPTER 9
DEALING WITH UNCHANGEABLE FAMILY ISSUES

Many hurting people coming to the church for help are dealing with an unchangeable issue in their family system which is constant and painful and creates a stress level that is difficult to manage. Biblical guidelines are presented to help a person cope with circumstances that will not change.

1. Acknowledge only God can change another person.
2. Be accountable to God for how you respond to others.
3. Concentrate on what you can change.
4. Pray specifically and in accordance with Scripture.
5. Develop a strong inner life of devotion.
6. Accept things as they are.
7. Acknowledge suffering isn't bad; it just hurts.
8. Stay connected to a Christian support system.
9. Maintain self-control.
10. Avoid "if only" thinking.
11. Be assertive and focused in applying your strategy.

Victorious living in the midst of trying circumstances can be a spiritual reality for all Christians.

CHAPTER 10
HELPING THE FINANCIALLY NEEDY

Merriam-Webster's Collegiate Dictionary defines *benevolence* as "a disposition to do good, an act of kindness, a generous gift."[1] In Proverbs we learn that "Whoever is kind to the needy honors God" (NIV). In this chapter, I describe the Casas benevolence ministry and the biblical basis for helping people financially. It is a story of how God blessed us because we honored him with our commitment to help people in financial crisis. During the last ten years, this ministry was blessed with $1,553,737 to give away to those in need. I discuss how different churches fund benevolence programs and the strengths and weaknesses of each method. Models for the administration of benevolence are presented and critiqued. Operational strategies are discussed with emphasis on the assessment process crucial to insure good stewardship is practiced. The importance of an integrated benevolence philosophy that addresses the total person and their needs in context with the life of the church and the community is highlighted. We have worked to avoid the "Band-Aid" approach and have sought to encourage those seeking financial help to connect to the body of Christ in relationally powerful ways. The fact that the benevolence fund is the third largest designated fund at Casas speaks to the importance this church has placed on extending a tangible expression of Christ's love and compassion to the needy.

CHAPTER 11
TAKING CARE OF YOURSELF

In writing to pastors in AD 591, Gregory admonished them to not ignore their own health in the process of healing others. Pastors have one of the most stressful jobs in our society. They often neglect their own physical, mental, and spiritual health. In this chapter, I share the lessons learned over the past twenty-five years by our staff in the care of our own souls and physical health. We have identified and experienced seven distinct stressors that are unique to the role of pastor. Included are:

▸ The awesome responsibility of "rightly dividing the word of truth" (2 Tim. 2:15, KJV)
▸ Time pressures in preparation for teaching and preaching responsibilities
▸ Multiple skill set demands
▸ Dealing with spiritual attacks
▸ Coping with high expectations
▸ Lower salaries
▸ Being on call
▸ The loneliness and isolation of leadership.

Strategies for effective coping are shared. I also discuss the need to address one's personal woundedness as part of establishing a healthy response to the stress of ministry. I point out that personal woundedness is often, in our experience, tragically overlooked by the pastor and those trying to help him as a significant contributor to ministerial burnout. Recommendations for healing the soul of the pastor are presented.

CHAPTER 12
TRENDS IN PASTORAL CARE

Six trends which will shape the way pastoral care is administered in the future are:

Recovery ministries

We live in a culture dominated by addictive and compulsive behaviors related to food, sex, money, alcohol, drugs, work, relationships, and the list goes on. Idolatry is the core spiritual issue present in addictive behavior. As churches, we have a responsibility to contribute to healthy recovery strategies by offering a biblical worldview perspective which addresses idolatry and the spiritual bondage it creates. Recovery will be a focal point of "soul care" in the twenty-first century. The existence of the Institute for Recovery Ministries at Fuller Seminary and degree programs in recovery ministries speaks powerfully to this trend.

Christian counseling

Christian Counseling has emerged as a recognized and accepted "adjunct" in the mental health field. The driving force behind its emergence is the fifty thousand-member American Association of Christian Counselors, which is defining the "profession" by promoting educational, ethical, and credentialing standards. Pastors have joined this organization and are making significant contributions to the process of raising the profile of Christian counseling as a profession. The partnership of pastor with counselor will continue to develop and shape pastoral care in this decade. Christian counselors will also be impacted by this interaction as they discuss the importance of spiritual formation, discipleship, and being connected to a community of believers.

Spiritual formation

There are many who are advocating that Christian counselors should be familiar with spiritual formation strategies that can be taught to clients as the means to spiritual maturity and intimacy with God. There are new degree programs being offered in spiritual formation and counseling that will connect theology and counseling theories and further promote the pastor-counselor dialog and cooperation.

Lay helping ministries

Many are predicting the explosion of lay helping ministries in the church. The growth of managed healthcare will continue to result in many being without mental health services. Churches will be called upon to provide services at no cost. Trained lay helpers will provide the manpower to meet this need. Given the need to be concerned about risk management, the training and supervision of lay ministries must be conducted with care.

Neurobiology and brain science

Science stands on the verge of major breakthroughs in our understanding of how the brain works and how to treat dysfunctions in brain chemistry. As one scientist put it, "the goal is to find penicillin for mental illness."[1] Many of the people we pray for and minister to will be relieved of their suffering. While most pastors and counselors would accept the notion that biology is not destiny, there will be challenges to theology and faith.

Professional licensure, risk management and Christian counseling

Churches that have professional counselors on staff will continue to face challenges related to following biblical guidelines and standards and at the same time being in compliance with state licensure requirements. One possible area of conflict is in what constitutes "professional behavior." Could the practice of Christian counseling be interpreted as engaging in activities as a licensee that are unprofessional by current standards of practice? These and other relevant questions are discussed with the assumption that we should approach the future of our relationships with licensure boards and the courts by establishing solid risk management procedures and maintain an attitude of confidence and faith.

NOTES

Chapter 1
Pastoral Care in Historical Perspective

1. St. Gregory, *Pastoral Care.* Ed. and trans. Henry Davis S. J. (Ancient Christian Writers) (Westminster, MD: The Newman Press, 1978), 92–232.

2. Ibid., 11–12.

3. Ibid., 11.

4. William A. Clebsh and Charles R. Jaekle, *Pastoral Care in Historical Perspective* (Northvale, NJ: Jason Aronson Inc., 1983), 87.

5. Ibid., 45.

6. Richard Baxter, *A Christian Directory*, 5th ed. (Morgan, PA: Soli Deo Gloria Publications, 1665), 4.

7. J. I. Packer, *A Christian Directory* (Morgan, PA: Soli Deo Gloria Publications, 1996), vii.

8. Clebsh and Jaekle, *Pastoral Care in Historical Perspective*, 8–10.

9. Ibid., 12.

10. Ibid., 13–14.

Chapter 2
A Contemporary Perspective: The Casas Story

1. Francis MacNutt, *The Nearly Perfect Crime: How the Church Almost Killed the Ministry of Healing* (Grand Rapids, MI: Chosen Books, 2005), 140.

2. William Barclay, *The Gospel of Matthew,* Vol. 1. (Philadelphia, PA: Westminster Press, 1958), 28.

3. Francis MacNutt, *The Nearly Perfect Crime: How the Church Almost Killed the Ministry of Healing* (Grand Rapids, MI: Chosen Books, 2005), 148.

4. Ibid., 150–151.

5. Ramsay MacMullen, *Christianizing the Roman Empire: AD 100–400* (London: Yale University Press, 1975), 21.

6. Roger Barrier, *The Kingdom and the Power.* Eds. Gary S. Greig and Kevin N. Springer. (Ventura, CA: Regal Books, 1993), 234.

7. Charles H. Kraft, *Confronting Powerless Christianity* (Grand Rapids, MI: Chosen Books, 2002), 37–39.

8. Neil T. Anderson, The Bondage Breaker (Eugene, OR: Harvest House, 1990).

Chapter 3
An Integrative Model: Healing Prayer and Counseling

1. Timothy M. Warner, *Spiritual Warfare* (Wheaton, IL: Crossway Books, 1991), 27.

2. William A. Clebsh and Charles R. Jaekle, *Pastoral Care in Historical Perspective* (Northvale, NJ: Jason Aronson Inc, 1983), 33.

3. Francis MacNutt, *The Nearly Perfect Crime: How the Church Almost Killed the Ministry of Healing* (Grand Rapids, MI: Chosen Books, 2005), 211–217.

Chapter 4
Helping Those in Spiritual Bondage

1. Roger Barrier, "Dealing With the Devil" Tuscon, Arizona, December 2, 2001.

2. Anderson, *The Bondage Breaker*.

3. Charles H. Kraft, *Confronting Powerless Christianity* (Grand Rapids, MI: Chosen Books, 2002), 212.

4. Neil T. Anderson, *Discipleship Counseling* (Ventura, CA: Regal Books, 2002), 11.

5. Neil T. Anderson, *Steps to Freedom in Christ* (Ventura, CA: Gospel Light, 2004), 6–20.

6. Ibid., 23.

Chapter 5
Helping Difficult People

1. American Psychiatric Association, *Quick Reference to Diagnostic Criteria: Diagnostic and Statistical Manual of Mental Disorders, Fourth Edition* (Washington, DC: APA), 275.

2. Richard P. Vaughn, *Pastoral Counseling and Personality Disorders* (Kansas City, MO: Sheed and Ward, 1994), 15–16.

3. Ibid, 76.

4. Ibid., 108.

Chapter 6
Helping Troubled Marriages

1. Barna Research Online: Christians and Divorce. www.barna.org (accessed November 9, 2002).

2. Mike McManus, *Marriage Savers* (Grand Rapids, MI: Zondervan, 1995).

Chapter 7
Helping the Addicted

1. U.S. Department of Health and Human Services. Substance Abuse and Mental Health Services Administration, 2002. Summary of Findings from the 2000 National Household Survey on Drug Abuse, Office of Applied Studies, NHSDA Series H-13 ed. (Washington, DC: U.S. Government Printing Office). Web site: www.samhsa.gov/oas/nhsda/chapter2.htm, accessed June 14, 2005.

2. Ibid.

3. Dale Ryan, "Recovery in the Church," *Steps* 14, No. 3 (2003): 3.

4. Ibid., 4–8.

5. Ibid., 6.

6. Andrew Kenny, *Teen Challenge's Proven Answer to the Drug Problem.* A review of a study by Dr. Aaron Bicknese: *The Teen Challenge Drug Treatment Program Comparative Perspective.*

(Unpublished doctoral dissertation, Northwestern University, Chicago, IL: 1994). Web site: www.teenchallengeusa.com, accessed November 16, 2006.

7. Patrick J. Carnes, *Out of the Shadows: Understanding Sexual Addiction* (Center City, MN: Hazelden, 1983), 12–13.

8. Al Cooper, "Sexuality and the Internet: Surfing into the New Millennium," *Cyberpsychology and Behavior* 1, no. 2 (1998): 181–187.

9. Carnes, *Out of the Shadows: Understanding Sexual Addiction*.

10. "The Leadership Survey," *Leadership Journal* Vol. 21 (2001): 89.

11. Mark R. Laaser and Louis J. Gregoire, "Pastors and Cybersex Addiction," *Sexual and Relationship Therapy* Vol. 3, No. 3 (2003): 18.

Chapter 8
Dealing with Distorted Images of God

1. Dale S. Ryan, "Recovery in the Church," *Steps* 14, 3–8.

2. J. B. Phillips, *Your God Is Too Small* (New York: The MacMillian Company, 1962), 54.

3. Neil Anderson and Tim Warner, *Beginners Guide to Spiritual Warfare* (Ann Arbor, MI: Servant Publications, 2000), 118.

Chapter 9
Dealing with Unchangeable Family Issues

1. Steven L. Dowdle, *Living with Unchangeable Family Issues* (unpublished document, 1996).

2. Mark I. Bubeck, *Spiritual Warfare Prayers* (pamphlet) (Chicago, IL: Moody Press, 1997).

3. Henry Blackaby and Claude V. King, *Experiencing God: Knowing and Doing His Will* (Nashville, TN: Lifeway Press, 1990).

Chapter 10
Helping the Financially Needy

1. *Merriam-Webster's Collegiate Dictionary*, 9th ed., s.v. "Benevolence."

Chapter 11
Taking Care of Yourself

1. St. Gregory, *Pastoral Care*, Ed. and trans. Henry Davis S.J. (Ancient Christian Writers) (Westminster, MD: The Newman Press, 1978), 234.

2. H.B. London and Neil B. Wiseman, *Pastors at Risk* (Wheaton, IL: Victor Books, 1993), 30.

3. Ibid., 172.

4. John C. LaRue Jr., "Profile of Today's Pastor: Ministry Ups and Downs," *Your Church*, July/August 1995, www.christianitytoday.com (accessed July 25, 2005).

5. London and Wiseman, *Pastors at Risk*, 30.

6. Ibid., 148.

7. Ibid., 148.

8. Ibid., 118.

9. John C. LaRue Jr., "Pastors at Work: Where the Time Goes," *Leadership Journal* January 2001, www.christianitytoday.com (accessed September 7, 2005).

10. "Is the Pastor's Family Safe at Home?" *Leadership Journal* Vol. 12, (1992): 38–44.

11. H. B. London Jr. and Neil B. Wiseman, *Pastors at Greater Risk* (Ventura, CA: Regal Books, 2003), 86.

12. Save America Ministries newsletter, Spring 2005. Web site: www.saveus.org/newsletter, accessed September 25, 2005.

13. London and Wiseman, *Pastors at Greater Risk*, 264.

14. Ibid., 238.

15. Charles R. Figley, Ed. Treating Compassion Fatigue (New York: Brummer-Routledge, 2002).

16. Roger Barrier, *Listening to the Voice of God* (Minneapolis, MN: Bethany House, 1998) 14.

Chapter 12
Trends in Pastoral Care

1. T. E. Clinton and George Ohlschlager (eds.), *Competent Christian Counseling* (Colorado Springs, CO: Waterbrook Press, 2002), 31.

2. G. R. Collins, "A Vision for Christian Counseling," *Christian Counseling Today* 3, no. 1 (1995): 8.

3. Clinton and Ohlschlager, *Competent Christian Counseling*, 697.

4. Collins, *The Biblical Basis of Christian Counseling for People Helpers*, 211.

5. Clinton and Ohlschlager, *Competent Christian Counseling*, 131.

6. Ibid.

7. Larry Crabb, *Connecting: Healing for Ourselves and our Relationships, A Radical New Vision*, (Nashville, TN: Word, 1997), xii.

8. Siang Yang Tan, "Lay Counseling: The State of the Art," *Christian Counseling Today* 7, No. 2 (1999): 32–34.

9. Everett L. Worthington, "Five Mega-Trends Affecting Christian Counseling," *Christian Counseling Connection*, No. 3 (2004): 1–9.

10. Nancy C. Andreasen, *Brave New Brain* (New York: Oxford University Press, 2001), ix.

11. T. E. Clinton and George Ohlschlager (eds.), *Competent Christian Counseling* (Colorado Springs, CO: Waterbrook Press, 2002), 140.

12. Nancy C. Andreasen, *Brave New Brain* (New York: Oxford University Press, 2001), 2–3.

13. Daniel G. Amen, "Healing the Hardware of the Soul," *Christian Counseling Today* 12, no. 3 (2004): 20.

14. Nancy C. Andreasen, *Brave New Brain* (New York: Oxford University Press, 2001), 4–5.

15. Everett L. Worthington, "Five Mega-Trends Affecting Christian Counseling," *Christian Counseling Connection*, No. 3 (2004): 1–9.

16. Arizona Revised Statutes R32-33:4-6, 101, Document, Arizona State Legislature, Phoenix, Arizona, July 1, 2004.

17. T. E. Clinton and George Ohlschlager (eds.), *Competent Christian Counseling* (Colorado Springs, CO: Waterbrook Press, 2002), 280.

Appendix A
Non-Christian Spiritual Experience Inventory

1. Neil T. Anderson, *The Steps to Freedom in Christ* (Ventura, CA: Gospel Light, 2004), 6.

Appendix B
Have You Ever...

1. Neil T. Anderson, *The Steps to Freedom in Christ* (Ventura, CA: Gospel Light, 2004), 7.

Appendix E
Casas Policy Statement on Idolatry

1. Policy statement of Casas Adobes Baptist Church, adopted May 9, 1996.

Appendix G
Casas Statement on Healthy Living:
Healing Our Dysfunctions

1. Roger Barrier, "Dealing With the Devil," Casis Church, Tuscon, Arizona, December 2, 2001.

Appendix H
Because God Loves Me

1. Web site: www.saddlebackfamily.com/smallgroups/faqs_resources.asp?id=7490, accessed December 5, 2006.

Chapter 1 Summary

1. J. I. Packer, *A Christian Directory* (Morgan, PA: Soli Deo Gloria Publications, 1665), 4.

Chapter 10 Summary

1. *Merriam-Webster's Collegiate Dictionary*, 9th ed., s.v. "Benevolence."

Chapter 12 Summary

1. Nancy C. Andreasen, *Brave New Brain* (New York: Oxford University Press, 2001), xi.

MINISTRY CONTACT INFORMATION

American Association of Christian Counselors
P.O. Box 739
Forest, VA 24551
1-800-526-8673
E-mail: memberservices@AACC.net

Celebrate Recovery
Saddleback Community Church
25422 Trabuco Rd. #105–151
Lake Forest, CA 92630
www.CelebrateRecovery.com

Center for Spirituality, Theology and Health
Duke University Medical Center and Divinity School
Durham, NC
E-mail: koenig@geri.duke.edu

Christian Association for Psychological Studies
P.O. Box 310400
New Braunfels, TX 78131-0400
830-629-2277
Fax: 830-629-2342
www.caps.net
E-mail: capsintl@compulvision.net

Christian Healing Ministries, Inc.
P.O. Box 9520
Jacksonville, FL 32208
904-765-3332
www.christianhealingmin.org

Church Initiative: Divorce Care, Grief Share,
Divorce Care for Kids, Before You Divorce
P.O. Box 1739
Wake Forest, NC 27588
1-800-395-5755
www.griefshare.org
E-mail: Churchmail1@aol.com

Crown Financial Ministries
P.O. Box 100
Gainesville, GA 305503
1-800-722-1976
www.crown.org

Focus on the Family
Pastoral Ministries Department
1-800-232-6459
www.parsonage.org
Pastoral Care Line 1-877-233-4455

Freedom in Christ Ministries
9051 Executive Park Drive Suite 503
Knoxville, TN 37923
Customer Service: 866-462-4747
Fax: 865-342-4001
Office: 865-342-4000
www.ficm.org
E-mail: info@ficm.org

Fuller Theological Seminary Institute for Christian Recovery
135 N Oakland Avenue
Pasadena, CA 91182
626-584-5200
www.fullerinstitute.org

National Association for Christian Recovery
P.O. Box 215
Brea, CA 2822
714-529-6227
Fax: 714-529-1120
www.christianrecovery.com

Pastoral Care Services
Casas Church
10801 N La Cholla Blvd.
Tucson, AZ 85742
520-742-5835
Fax: 520-878-1229
E-mail: steved@casaschurch.org

Stone Gate Resources
11509 Palmer Divide Rd.
Larkspur, CO 80118
888-575-3030/303-688-5680
www.stonegateresources.org
Harry Schaumburg, author of *False Intimacy: Understanding the Struggle of Sexual Addiction*

Heart to Heart Counseling Center
P.O. Box 51055
Colorado Springs, CO 80947
719-278-3708
www.sexaddict.com
Douglas Weiss, author of *101 Practical Exercises: A Christian Guide for Sexual Addiction Recovery*